First World War
and Army of Occupation
War Diary
France, Belgium and Germany

50 DIVISION
151 Infantry Brigade
King's Royal Rifle Corps
4th Battalion
1 July 1918 - 7 June 1919

WO95/2843/3

The Naval & Military Press Ltd
www.nmarchive.com
Published in association with The National Archives

Published by

The Naval & Military Press Ltd

Unit 10 Ridgewood Industrial Park,

Uckfield, East Sussex,

TN22 5QE England

Tel: +44 (0) 1825 749494

www.naval-military-press.com

www.nmarchive.com

This diary has been reprinted in facsimile from the original. Any imperfections are inevitably reproduced and the quality may fall short of modern type and cartographic standards.

© Crown Copyright
Images reproduced by permission of The National Archives, London, England, 2015.

Contents

Document type	Place/Title	Date From	Date To
Heading	WO95/2843/3 4 Bn. King's Royal Rifle Corps 1919 July-1919 June		
Heading	50th Division 151st Infy Bde 4th Bn K.R.R. Corps Jly 1918-Jun 1919 Form Salonika 27 Dn. 80 Bde.		
War Diary	Serqueux	01/07/1918	14/07/1918
War Diary	Arques Martin-Eglise	15/07/1918	15/07/1918
War Diary	Martin-Eglise	16/07/1918	17/07/1918
Miscellaneous	Appendix "B" List of Casualties for the month of July, 1918.		
Heading	War Diary 4th Bn. Kings Royal Rifle Corps. August 1918 Volume-IV		
War Diary	Martin-Eglise. Dieppe 1/100,000	10/08/1918	30/08/1918
Miscellaneous	Appendix "B" List of Casualties for the Month of August, 1918.		
Heading	War Diary 4th Kings Royal Rifle Corps September, 1918 Volume-IV No. 10		
War Diary	Martin Eglise (Dieppe 1/100,000)	01/09/1918	16/09/1918
War Diary	Beaudricourt (Lens 1/100,000)	16/09/1918	24/09/1918
War Diary	Bertangles (Amiens 1/100,000)	25/09/1918	26/09/1918
War Diary	Bertangles	27/09/1918	27/09/1918
War Diary	Nurlu (Valenciennes (1/100,000)	28/09/1918	30/09/1918
Heading	War Diary 4th Bn Kings Royal Rifle Corps. October, 1918. Volume-IV No. 11		
War Diary	Epehy	01/10/1918	01/10/1918
War Diary	Bony	02/10/1918	02/10/1918
War Diary	Lecatalet	03/10/1918	03/10/1918
War Diary	Hindenburg Line No X Bony	04/10/1918	04/10/1918
War Diary	High Ground in A4a.xb. No./R Escaut.	04/10/1918	04/10/1918
War Diary	Hindenburg Line. N of Bony	05/10/1918	05/10/1918
War Diary	Vendhuile	06/10/1918	07/10/1918
War Diary	T.25.d. Near Guisancourt Farm	07/10/1918	08/10/1918
War Diary	Ref 57B 1/40,000	08/10/1918	08/10/1918
War Diary	Aubencheul	09/10/1918	09/10/1918
War Diary	Maretz	10/10/1918	16/10/1918
War Diary	St Souplet	17/10/1918	18/10/1918
War Diary	Avelu	19/10/1918	27/10/1918
War Diary	Maurois	29/10/1918	30/10/1918
Miscellaneous	Appendix "B" List of Casualties for the Month of October, 1918.		
Operation(al) Order(s)	4th Battalion, The King's Royal Rifle Corps. Operation Order No. 191		
Operation(al) Order(s)	4th Battalion, The King's Royal Rifle Corps. Operation Order No. 192.	16/10/1918	16/10/1918
Miscellaneous	4th Battalion, The King's Royal Rifle Corps. Appendix B.		
Miscellaneous	4th. Battalion, The King's Royal Rifle Corps.		
Heading	War Diary 4th Bn Kings Royal Rifle Corps November, 1918 Volume-IV No. 12		
War Diary	Lecateau	01/11/1918	08/11/1918
War Diary	St Remy Chaussee	09/11/1918	14/11/1918

Operation(al) Order(s)	4th Battalion, The King's Royal Rifle Corps. Operation Order No. 193	02/11/1918	02/11/1918
Miscellaneous	4th Battalion, The King's Royal Rifle Corps.		
Miscellaneous	Appendix 'B' Total Casualties for month ended 30th November, 1918		
Miscellaneous	3rd November to 9th November, 1916	03/11/1918	03/11/1918
War Diary	St Remy Chaussee	15/11/1918	30/11/1918
Heading	War Diary. 4th Bn. Kings Royal Rifle Corps December 1918 Vol IV		
War Diary	Dompierre	01/12/1918	10/12/1918
War Diary	Amfroipret	11/12/1918	30/12/1918
Heading	War Diary 4th Bn. King's Royal Rifle Corps January 1919 Vol 5 No. 2		
War Diary	Lalongueville	01/01/1919	31/01/1919
Heading	War Diary. 4th Bn. The Kings Royal Rifle Corps. 1st West February, 1919 Volume V. No. 3		
War Diary	La Longueville	10/02/1919	21/02/1919
War Diary	Jolimetz	21/02/1919	24/02/1919
War Diary	Jolimetz	13/02/1919	30/03/1919
War Diary	Jolimetz	07/03/1919	07/06/1919

WO 95 2843/3

4 Bn. King's Royal Rifle Corps

1918 JULY — 1919 JUNE

50TH DIVISION
151ST INFY BDE

4TH BN K. R. R. CORPS
JLY 1918-JUN 1919

FROM SALONIKA 27 DIV. 80 BDE

4th Batt. The KRRC

WAR DIARY
INTELLIGENCE SUMMARY

Army Form C. 2118.

Turkey 1918   Vol IV   No. 8

Place	Date	Hour	Summary of Events and Information	Remarks and references to Appendices
	July 1918 1st (SF)		En route from SALONIKA to FRANCE. Halted for meals at SAVOIE & VENTIMIGLIA (Italy) & CANNES (FRANCE)	(W.D.)
	2nd		"MIRAMAS" (very few amenities on trip). Dinner train places. In meals at PARIS, LE MONTAL, MALESHERBES, LE TRÉEL, ST GERMAIN & VERSAILLES.	(W.D.)
	3rd		Returned ARQUE LES EAUX (DIEPPE /100,000) 2 trains. The 7 miles to camp at SERQUEUX will about 8 officers & men.	(W.D.)
SERQUEUX	5th–13th		Was trying as the hats were offr/sgt at mines bases. In camp at SERQUEUX. Worked at my line water future was spent in rigging things up — lectures lathes for speeches as there was little chances to arrange for leave while in climate to but... to limit... special of OR ride to the and offr ... a day on ... train for ... a day sports to last for 28 days.	(E.A.N.) (W.D.)
	14th		Baths on inspected by G.O.C. IV Corps.	(W.D.)
ARQUES	15th 13th		Batts to ATTD corp whaineh at SERQUEUX/mdranuing at ARQUES 430 bm. ..... 3 miles to count at MARTIN EGLISE	

MARTIN EGLISE

Place	Date	Hour	Summary of Events and Information	Remarks and references to Appendices
MARTIN - EQUISE	16th		Remainder of Battn (greater [illegible]) arrived at MARTIN EQUISE. The Battalion is brigaded with 1st KOYLI & 2 INNISKILLING FUSILIERS in the 151ST Bde (Brig. Gen. TE SUGDEN) 50th Div (Maj-Gen HC JACKSON) KMP.	
	17th - 31st		Training & work in camp. There was little to relieve the monotony of the camp & the tents had to be dug down 2ft as protection against air raids. The weather was cold & stormy & men are Bn 29th when it became possible to let the 29th & the have to leave to the UK was put in the Army at 28 days.	
			Strength of Battn 1st July 33 Officers 658 OR 31st " 31 " 656 "	
			No drafts received. Battn was down to war grown healt of the Battn this worth is very good	

Signed [illegible] Maj R FC
Comdg 1 W/BN

Appendix "B"

List of Casualties for the month of JULY, 1918.

N I L.

Total Casualties to date:-

	Killed.	Wounded.	W & M.	Missing.	Died of Wounds.
Officers	6	34	1	3	1
Other Ranks.	192	639	6	237	8

No 3

WAR DIARY.

4th Bn. King's Royal Rifle Corps.

August 1918.

Volume — IV. N.9.

4 TB. The K.R.R.C. AUGUST 1918

Army Form C. 2118.

WAR DIARY
INTELLIGENCE SUMMARY

Vol IV No 9

Place	Date	Hour	Summary of Events and Information	Remarks and references to Appendices
MARTIN-EGLISE	August 1918			
DIEPPE 1/100,000			This month was spent in camp at MARTIN-EGLISE training, working on the camp. B.T.R. were much depleted by leave in the half the Battalion being away all the month. The Bn is still very much under strength in men - only one draft of 17 being received & a few men returning from Hospital. A large number of young Officers joined during the month. The heat at Dieppe while at FORET D'ARQUES has been very trying. (8 in camp) (Bn Capt) (Bn Capt) (Bn Capt)	
	10th			
	14th		12 new officers (1 an 2Lt) joined from England. (8 in camp)	
	16th		Brigade Tactical Scheme starting 3 a.m. invited guests present of King E. of	
	22nd		C.O. (Major GA Taylor MC) (8 in camp)	
			AMIENS.	
	26th		3 new officers (newly - 2 2Lts) joined. (8 in camp)	
	30th		Brigade night attack manoeuvre.	
			Strength of Battalion on 1st August 31 Officers 656 O.R.	
			" " " 31st " 45 " 671 "	
			The health of the Battalion this month was good.	

W.H. Major
The K.R.R.Corps
Comdg 4 Bn.

Appendix "B"

List of Casualties for the Month of August, 1918.

Accidentally Wounded, 23.8.18.   6/4972 Rfn. Gearing, G.

Total Casualties to date:-

	Killed.	Wounded.	W & M.	Missing.	Died of Wounds.
Officers	6	34	1	8	1
Other Ranks.	102	690	6	887	8

WAR DIARY

4th Kings Royal Rifle Corps

September, 1918

Volume — IV — No. 10.

4th Bn The King's Royal Rifle Corps WAR DIARY
INTELLIGENCE SUMMARY

SEPTEMBER 1918 Army Form C. 2118.
VOL IV   No 10.

Place	Date	Hour	Summary of Events and Information	Remarks and references to Appendices
MARTIN EGLISE (DIEPPE 1/100,000)	1st 4th 6th		Battalion Camp Training. Divisional Route March 13 miles. Divisional Tactical Exercise — No one fell out. Agreeing on a tape. dather from GREGES to BERNEVAL (DIEPPE 1/100,000) Arrived at BER in camp 3 pm. A draft of 200 OR joined from 6 Res Battn C.L.R (Blackdown) These men had all been evacuated from SALONIKA early in the year with malaria. They were all 4th Battalion men.	(RunCapt) (RunCapt before) (RunCapt)
	12th		Divisional Tactical exercise in embarkation of Bn & Carr Bn, Batt returned to camp about 3pm. Key were at Kat of the 65th ind.	(RunCapt) (RunCapt FILM CAPt)
	13th 15th		The Battalion entrained at MERI Station 1.30 am and 4 other officers which was left behind together with Copr Rd. TYNTER M.C. and 4 other officers retrained at BEAUCRICOURT (LENS 1/100,000) at Marched to billets at BEAUCRICOURT - five miles. The division is in XVII K CORPS.	(RunCapt)
BEAUCRICOURT (LENS 1/100,000)	17th		A draft of 100 OR received from 6 RKRB C.L.R. These were also men from SALONIKA, mostly old 3rd Batt men.	(RunCapt)
	17/24 2nd 1st 26th		Training at BEAUCRICOURT. Lt Col BRADY D.S.O. joined from 1st KRRC & assumed command of the Bn. Issued received who of unknown to fighting with RunCapt. BnPowen who of unknown to BERTANGLES arrived 2.30pm	(RunCapt) (RunCapt)
BERTANGLES (AMIENS 1/100,000)			The Bn then moved by bus to BERTANGLES where our Transport arose by march at midnight.	(RunCapt)

WAR DIARY
or
INTELLIGENCE SUMMARY.

(Erase heading not required.)

Army Form C. 2118.

Place	Date	Hour	Summary of Events and Information	Remarks and references to Appendices
BERTANGLES	27th		Transport moved by road to FRICOURT - MAMETZ AREA (AMIENS 1/100,000) Battalion was warned to be ready to move in the evening but this was cancelled for the night. Battalion remained in BERTANGLES.	(K.W.R.)
NURLU (VALENCIENNES 1/100,000)	28th	11.30 p.m.	Batt'n entrained at MERELLES vid AMIENS, ALBERT, MAMETZ, COMBLES to MOISLAINS (ref AMIENS 1/100,000) During the last two hours of our journey my kitchen caught fire. The rails were levered at this point about 2 miles. Finally arrived at our _____ about 9 a.m. and started away for the night. The Brigade by this time were _____ in Corps. Reserve.	(K.W.R.)
	29th		Battn remained in bivouac. Enemy were coming several times during the day. Interesting orders to move were issued later. Rain was dumped & the Battn proceeded by Company wagon in marching fighting order. shortly after arrival at _____ _____ who very shortly came back. Mount throughout heavy.	(K.W.R.)
	30th		Strength of the Battalion on 1st September 45 Officers O.R. 952 " " " " 30th " 47 " " " "	

Lieut. Col.
T.C. REBANK
Commanding 1/4th

15/50

Bn.
4th King's Royal Rifle Corps

WAR DIARY. Vol. 5

October, 1918.

Volume — IV. No. 11.

4th Bn: The Kings Royal Rifle Corps

WAR DIARY
or
INTELLIGENCE SUMMARY.
(Erase heading not required.)

Army Form C. 2118.

October 1918   VOL IV   No 11

Place	Date	Hour	Summary of Events and Information	Remarks and references to Appendices
EPEHY	1st		Ref MONTBREHAIN E.41.A 1/20,000	
			The Battalion left BOOMERANG WOOD (N17.d.) at 1600 hrs & moved into support line at EPEHY. (8th Corps Tpt & Pack Hp to B in LEMPIRE (St QUENTIN 1/40,000)	
BONY	2nd		Awning received homeline BSF, 42d & 44d. Battns Australians arrived in the line same evening. The C.O. (Capr HAYHURST-FRANCE), O.C. D Coy (Capt B BRADY), O.C. B Coy (Capt NUTTING) & O.C. A Coy (Capt HAYHURST-FRANCE) proceeded along ass bus to reco-noitred Australian Infantry Battns concerned & arranged details of relief. They involved taking over sectors of front & support lines from weak Australian Infantry Battns in true front line, not being kingliness of Battns in true front line, no time was available for any reconnaissance of line beyond Hdqrs of Battns concerned.	
		1700 hrs	Battalion marched from EPEHY, via L'EMPIRE, Ruins to N of BONY whence Australian guides met companies	
		2000 hrs	relief reported complete. Dispositions of Batts were as under:	
			"A" company (Lieut N.J.C. MACAULAY) In support about A.16.c.0. to 0.b.	A.15.d.b.0. " 6.7.
			"C" company (Lieut H.T. PREECE) in reserve " A.16.a.9.2. " 9.8.
			"D" company (Capt F.H. HAYHURST-FRANCE MC) in front line " A.10.c.0.0. " b.0.
			"B" company (Capt A.F. NUTTING MC) " " "
			Battalion Headquarters A.21.a.9.4.	

Army Form C. 2118.

WAR DIARY
or
INTELLIGENCE SUMMARY.   PAGE 2
(Erase heading not required.)

Instructions regarding War Diaries and Intelligence Summaries are contained in F.S. Regs., Part II. and the Staff Manual respectively. Title pages will be prepared in manuscript.

Place	Date	Hour	Summary of Events and Information	Remarks and references to Appendices
BONY.	2nd	2100 hrs	Phone message received from Brigade "Lt. BRADY to report forthwith to Bde H.Q. at F.17.d.7.2." On arrival Brigadier explained to Battalion Commanders plan for major operation to be carried out by Brigade at dawn on 3rd October in conjunction with attack by 2nd AUSTRALIAN Infantry on RIGHT and 14th Infantry Bde on LEFT. 1st Battalion was allotted the task of clearing the villages of LE CATALET and GOUY of the enemy and consolidating high ground N of LE CATALET village W of LE CATALET TRENCH in A.5.b. Battalion orders to 2 I/C B. for Liberation issued	Further orders were attd. Order 191
LE CATALET	3rd	0015 hrs	Very great difficulty was experienced in moving companies to positions of assembly. (Order 191, para 4). The ground was entirely unknown to guides were available. The night was dark with heavy thunderstorms & rain.	
		0530 hrs	Battalion Headquarters moved forward to A.15.b.9.3.	
		0550 hrs	Attacking companies reported in position of assembly.	
		0605 hrs	ZERO HOUR. Companies advanced to the attack	
		0730 hrs	First message received from Capt NUTTING O.C. "B" (Left) Coy reported attack progressing favorably, casualties heavy, reinforcements required.	
		0740 hrs	2nd platoon "C" Coy under Lieut DAVIES, were sent forward to reinforce B Coy (Capt NUTTING)	
		0830 hrs	Second message from Capt NUTTING, B Coy times 0740 hrs asked for further help as company reduced to 30 rifles & encountering heavy M.G. fire.	
		0840 hrs	Lieut PREECE with Howard M.G. Hqs Coy 2 platoons to reinforce CAPT NUTTING.	

WAR DIARY or INTELLIGENCE SUMMARY

Army Form C. 2118.

Page 3

Place	Date	Hour	Summary of Events and Information	Remarks and references to Appendices
LE CATELET	3	0900 hrs	Capt HAYHURST-FRANCE commanding "D" (Right Flank) Coy reported LE CATELET un-tenanted at Battalion Headquarters, and reported Coy N. of LE CATELET cleared the enemy from dugouts on high ground N. of LE CATELET but encountering heavy M.G. fire from front & right flanks. He relieved Lieut MACAULY (missing since) who had also been wounded. By this time (0900) units had become scattered and somewhat disorganised owing to severe nature of fight although the villages were of little importance & inadequately understood. Enemy kept on to heavy losses incurred. The task of the Coy. was therefore most unfortunate. An advance 2000 yds long N. of the village had produced from no information. All Lewis gun teams appearing beyond N. outskirts of LE CATELET came at once under heavy M.G. fire mostly from the sunken road in A.4.c.3.3 which was not well dealt with by left Brigade. — from trenches of Reichsten commanding guns in S.28.d. Troops holding dug in on outskirts of villages N.W & N.E. Gaining approach from N as far as practicable.	
		1130am	Considerable parties of the enemy were observed about this time working their way towards the outskirts of GOUY down the valley in S.30 turning towards front line & heavy casualties taken. 4th Battn. was then two miles to North any determined counter attack. A company of 5 NORTHUMBERLAND FUSILIERS placed at disposal of Battalion, who though relieved were up a position in support in A.11.c.d. below a Reserve Company of N.F. was ordered to take up position in A.11.c. in auxiliaries commanded by Lieut Wright.	
		1300M	LE CATELET persisted by enemy. Our artillery again opened harassing in NE of LE CATELET but result too effective to enable N up the VALLEY in S.30 into GOUY was further towards	

Army Form C. 2118.

WAR DIARY
or
INTELLIGENCE SUMMARY. Page 4

(Erase heading not required.)

Instructions regarding War Diaries and Intelligence Summaries are contained in F. S. Regs., Part II. and the Staff Manual respectively. Title pages will be prepared in manuscript.

Place	Date	Hour	Summary of Events and Information	Remarks and references to Appendices
LE CATALET	3		Tesemweilleuve, nong to houses my fire from enemy MG's from vantage ground around village, was practically unhampson in daylight and details of situation and dispositions remained obscured until evening when both VILLAGES were found to be still clear of the enemy.	
		2930 hu	At this hour Battalion was relieved by 1st R. MUNSTER FUSILIERS & withdrew to HINDENBURG LINE of BONY about A.15.a. Casualties 3 killed, 6 wounded. Officers Other Ranks killed 1 off. 252. OR. wounded 35. 5 missing	
			Prisoners Captured — Machine guns captured — The enemy fought with a determination which has seldom been witnessed. Both ranks & officers fought his captured positions through woods & week of MG's & rifles every way of approach & snipers from the upper windows of houses commanded every street. The tank broke the Battalion into for very resolute leading, individual initiative & resourcefulness between ... & very of ... within the Regiment demand that ... in the Battalion will duly with that untiring accuracy & determined courage ... A Regiment demands ...	*(initialled)*
HINDENBURG LINE N of BONY	4	0900 hu	Relieved from Bres relieved Batten placing Battalion are B.G.C. 150 INF BDE	

Army Form C. 2118.

WAR DIARY
or
INTELLIGENCE SUMMARY.
(Erase heading not required.)

page 5

Place	Date	Hour	Summary of Events and Information	Remarks and references to Appendices
HINDENBURG LINE N of BONY	4th	1100 hrs	Muled received to hold the line of the ESCAUT RIVER from MACQUINCOURT FARM (A.3.d) to QUINCAMP MILL (A.4.d) together with such gap which was then known to exist between Canal & LE CATALET VILLAGE. An immediate reconnaissance carried out by Capt NUTTING & Lieut BENNETT (Int Off) established that the British troops still held the line of MARQUIVAL FARM (exclusive) to outskirts of LE CATALET and that MARQUIVAL FARM being still in the enemy's hands. Two Coys were forthwith sent forward to hold the line of the River (viz 2 + 3 Coys) and were ripter on under B Company in TRENCH running through A.9.b + A.10.a, with posts pushed forward to river work. C Company along the living of man in A.10.a. with posts pushed forward to RIVER BANK. A & D Companies in reserve at A.9.c. C Coys position were subjected to frequent bursts of enemy fire & heavy T M fire during the day & this company suffered some casualties. B Coy much interfered.	
		12 noon	During the afternoon the line A.3.a. to A.4.d. which was found to be arrived at irregular intervals by four single plank bridges, 20 feet wide suggesting an average depth of 3 to 4 feet	
		17.00 hrs	14th Bty pushed forward to Huts 150 yd Rd (A.21.b.1.9) to report situation (probably this reconnaissance he found several parties of enemy along trail then to move Batt to this portion	

Army Form C. 2118.

WAR DIARY
or
INTELLIGENCE SUMMARY.

Page 5

(Erase heading not required.)

Place	Date	Hour	Summary of Events and Information	Remarks and references to Appendices
HINDENBURG LINE M.O BONY	4		Multiple explosions apparently along Road by A4 a.10 staffeker at dump at S.28.C. The enemy system of snipers posts on the high ground in A.4.b & S.28.c. Thather was to be canned out when Lt Col BRADY's command by elements of ROYAL FUSILIERS then relieved its positions after sundown was in A45 & little role in support. After was to be more without artillery support. If opposition to Lt Col BRADY's advance were to be suspected to heavy bombardment prior to capture, prior where to be strictly unretaliated. If opposition to the Battalion was to be relieved then annihilation reported. Two companies were ordered to A+D coys to move forward patrols to intermediate Sudden Road in A.4 a.9. Lt Col BRADY was attached to Headquarters BGC coys 2/Marines Situation dismal there coys forward in A.4.a.4b.	
High Ground at A.4 a.4b N.|ll ESCAUT.		1825 hrs 1830 hrs	B&C coys reported in position. Liaison officers of Royal Fusiliers reported to be LtBRADY that he shortly no men would have proper towards Lt BRADY while decided to carry but the other with the 4th K.R.R.Y.C. between all elements of ROYAL FUSILIERS to clear the main civilians to Quarry about A.4.C. central. Disposition for either were then made of newly communicating disposition in either were then made of newly communicating reconnassance, C Coy (Lieut H.T. PREECE) Headquarters & outposts. Enemy had withdrawn. Position S.28. C 97. & A.4.a.7.2. B+A coys (Capt A F NUTTING) to capture & consolidate enemy System about S.28.d.74 Coy (Lt B ERSHAM) to remain on main Road in A.4 a.4b close support.	

WAR DIARY
or
INTELLIGENCE SUMMARY.

Army Form C. 2118.

Page 7

Place	Date	Hour	Summary of Events and Information	Remarks and references to Appendices
High ground N of ESCAUT	4	1905 hrs	An Enemy reported infantry concentration & continuous volumes of artillery fire to our front. These two coys moving up artillery formation new Ypres ground, then in A.10.a. suffered some casualties.	
		1915 hrs	Which was punished. Enemy driven in stomach for fight will resistance was encountered & thrown back.	
		2045 hrs	Machine guns & ammunition were reported by 2045 hrs, prisoners were HARZ prisoners of some 26 MGs + 2 TMs 2 officers and 57 men. 2 TMs captures. Casualties suffered by Battalion very light.	
			Telephone connected to Signal Station of 150 Inf Bde was not manually. Battalion Signals succeeded in keeping up 149 Inf Bde Hqrs by LUCAS LAMP. Intercom with Bns was communicated to 150 Bde Hqrs by Battalion runners. (Dr Law) 2Staff.	
HINDENBURG LINE, N of BONY	5	0400 hrs	which was relieved by 2 Staff. Y Su Bouvering at 0400 hrs tried Several offensive of this operation were known by the eng commenced by his artillery workers like which the eng commenced by shell which Assembly on high tree from early over Operations on the position. Without any previous reconnaissance movements of wounded not have been carried at by show their highly developed system. An enemy fresh ran away mining to the infantry towards with shell fire what over was launched.	A.D. Bill

A 3834 Wt: W4973/M687 750,000 8/16 D.D. & L. Ltd. Forms/C.2118/13

WAR DIARY or INTELLIGENCE SUMMARY

Army Form C. 2118.

PAGE 8

Place	Date	Hour	Summary of Events and Information	Remarks and references to Appendices
VENDHUILE	6	1000hrs	Moved to VENDHUILE where Bn was concentrated in tents, dugouts & cellars. Bn HQ. S.26.c.3.2.	
Ref Sheet 57B	8	0500 hrs	1/20,000 Received Bn Tpt & near HQ.	ENEMY
		0600	O.C. moved to TRIPOT WOD VENDHUILE on LEMPIRE ROAD with A.D. to position of Bn HQ where issued in general instructions.	
			In A.b.D. C.O. + Coy Comdrs to meet B.g.C at 1830 hrs at Rd junction in A.b.D. when details of operation in which 8th Battalion was to take part which was issued in provisional form moving of 8th would be communicated	
	1800hrs		Where he in position as above.	
	1900hrs		Here verbal orders issued by B.g.C operations at unknown hour an 8th mBan'g, from a defensive flour (facing N) to left flank of 6th Division attacking in N.E. direction.	
		At 05.20 hrs	(a) Left boundary of 8th Division GUISANCOURT FARM (exclusive) to T.27 central to MARLICHES FARM (inclusive).	
			(b) The 4" KRRC to advance at ZERO from position with left attacking Bn of 8th Division.	
			(c) 38th Division to attack simultaneously N of MILLERS OUTREAUX through	
		T.10	in S.E. direction.	
			(d) Whole of Rifle Bde & Right Bn 38th Div. to envelop MARLICHES FM.	
		(e)	Trench of 4 KRRC not to advance beyond MARLICHES FM.	
		(f)	Tanks to be established by 4 KRRC at position as under:	
			A per above T.2.b.B.9.9.	] C.Coy
			B " T.2.1.b.0.7.J	
			C " T.22.c.2.9.J	D Coy
			D " T.22.a.0.3.J	
			E per above T.1.b.a.4.2.	] A Coy
			F " " MARLICHES FM (T.17.c.)	

Army Form C. 2118.

WAR DIARY
or
INTELLIGENCE SUMMARY.
(Erase heading not required.)

Page 9.

Place	Date	Hour	Summary of Events and Information	Remarks and references to Appendices
T.25.d. Near GUISANCOURT FARM.	7		(1) Assembly positions of 4 KRRC MASMIERES - BEAUREVOIR Trenches from T.20 central to T.26.d.4.6. Barrage line T.21.c.2.0. - Try central - advancing 100 yds every 5 minutes. In 3 successive waves of companies in Fneration. Advance in 3 successive waves of companies in section of platoons front at 400 yards. Each platoon in Artillery formation.	
		22.00 hrs.	(i) ZERO 05.20 hrs.	
		23.50 hrs.	Battalion moved to positions of assembly (View 9)) with Batt HQ about sunken road in T.26.a. Batt reported in position. Thereupon was carried out with the rapidity owing to excellent guides provided by Scottish Horse.	E.M.A.P.
	8	01.00 hrs.	Assembly position was carried out by two coys of 1 KOYLI resulting in capture of VILLERS FARM in T.20.b. In reply enemy attacked but mortary barrage on Assembly positions of 4 KRRC. Left of attacking Batts of 65th Division the Batts suffered some 10 casualties left.	
		05.20 hrs.	Two A coy advanced to the attack in three waves with left whacking Batt of 66th Division.	
		06.20 hrs.	Message received from "C" Coy (timed 05.20 hrs) to say line - TREECE had been taken; "A" port scratched entrance to "B" port without opposition.	
		07.10 hrs. 08.00 hrs.	going to heavy MG fire. Message timed 06.50 hrs from "C" Coy, referred to "B" Battalion position, ("C" "D" "B"), ("C" "D" "B").	

WAR DIARY
or
INTELLIGENCE SUMMARY.

Page 10.

Place	Date	Hour	Summary of Events and Information	Remarks and references to Appendices
	8.	0815hrs	but were to maintain his troops there trying to very heavy M.G. fire. Company their intentions about T.22. central.	
		1030hrs	message from "A" coy reported Batts of 66 Inf. Div. had reached MARLICHE'S FARM but had been compelled to withdraw again. Towers have been sent after to deal with situation. Leaving platoon of "A" coy had also the withdrawn some 300 yds to conform with his withdrawing Batts of 66 Division.	
			2 Lieut BENNETT (B. With. offer) who had led advance of "A" coy's company having returned to B. HQrs. + reported "A" coy in posn in bck ctrd, "E" poy established by "A" coy but advance to MARLICHE'S FARM held up by M.G. next south. Lieut RAYNAM, army "A" coy, 2 Lieut MUNTON comg A coy, Lieut CORSBY + 2Lt AUSTIN, H.K.-A- coy, had been wounded.	
		1100hrs	The C.O. + OC B coy (Capt NUTTING) made reconnaissance of situation up to vicinity of PETIT VERGER FARM. Progress very difficult owing to M.G. fire from VILLERS OUTREAUX + continuous shelling of old German between GUIBEYCOURT FARM + PETIT VERGER FARM away of which appeared to be under direct observation from high ground about U.7. central.	
		1200hrs	B. With. officer accompanied by Capt MILLER (Adjutant) proceeded to MARLICHE'S FARM in order to ascertain the situation there. Which found quiet. 2/5 Div. having gone through there north. Another Cape MILLER + B. With. officer entered the from new of the enemy paper showing that	

Place	Date	Hour	Summary of Events and Information	Remarks and references to Appendices
	8	1.50 hrs 11 pm	Battalion reorganised & withdrawn to VAUX HALL QUARRY. Battn moved to WIEKS in AUBENCHEUL. Casualties in this operation: 1 Officer killed, 4 Officers wounded, 12 OR " , 40 OR " Captures: 2 Officers 111 OR prisoners 1 77mm Field Gun 4 Machine guns. Into history of the Battalion the chief difficulties of the operation are as under. (1) Very short notice received of proposed attack, no experience in such advance possible in daylight, troops moved into attacking positions in the dark throughout. (2) Infantry Battalion on our right flank (HIGHLAND L.I.) was of the VILLERS OUTREAUX and our guarding army was thereby completely exposed. This village afforded invaluable cover for return of enemy M.G.'s and snipers of which immense numbers were made any use of. (3) The whole of the ground reconnoitred advance by Batt'n was under heavy observation of enemy from high ground. The numbers of enemy unoccupied M.G.'s shortly manned & very carefully sited, which had to be overrun during progress of advance. (in some 3 Officers 141 ORS surrendered with 5 MGs). If the actual fighting - in different bogey war in which thick	

WAR DIARY or INTELLIGENCE SUMMARY

Army Form C. 2118. Page 12

Place	Date	Hour	Summary of Events and Information	Remarks and references to Appendices
Tr/51B/40,000			but the enemy resistance succeeded in holding up our attack for any appreciable degree, nor positions of the enemy tr. were definitely located. The positions made by officers & n.c.o.'s to deal with emergency situations as they arose, were successful without exception — in fact the very fine work of Lt. Kymer & Serj. Jeeves specially deserved. The inspection situation created by delay of troops on left flank of Battn. in clearing VILLERS OUTREAUX was wholly beyond control of Lt. Battn. The situation turn age with which an reached carried out their work here with the face of the difficulties enumerated above again shows fr. the Battalion an expression of warmest appreciation fr. the Corps Commander Sir T. MORLAND, fr. Major General JACKSON commanding the 50th Division, fr. Brig. General Sq GEN commanding 151 Iy Bde.	Enclosed
AUBENCHEUL	9"		Nothing of sighting - Capt G.B. ESDEN joined Bn. from Bn. as a coy.	Enclosed
MARETZ	10"		Marched at 0745 hrs to GOUY & Then to MARETZ.	
	11"		BEAUREVOIR, ELINCOURT & CLARY to MARETZ. Battn. went into excellent billets. Two officers joined from Base. The following announcements came from junior officers C.O. on work of Battn.	Enclosed

WAR DIARY or INTELLIGENCE SUMMARY

Army Form C. 2118.

Page 13.

Place	Date	Hour	Summary of Events and Information	Remarks and references to Appendices
MARETZ	12		Battle surplus returned Batt: from BERTANGLES near AMIENS. Parade for individual immediate (M/General JACKSON). He congratulated Batt: on their good work.	
	13th		Move into billeting area on S. side of LE CATEAU ROAD. (EUNAPT)	
	14-15th		Move up — having fixed to take part in major operation commencing 1145hrs on the 17th. Batt: Officers were to make a daylight reconnaissance A.O. + Bn. Commanders of enemy positions near ST SOUPLET.	see attached O.O. 192
		1508hrs	Batt: paraded 190 other ranks in BUSIGNY to proceed to ESCAUFORT which had been found in Q.27.d. Batt: proceeded to positions opposite their attack	VIDE DETAILED ACCOUNT ATTACHED
		1900hrs		
ST SOUPLET	17th	0005hrs	Patrol sent near SELLE by men in greatly outnumbered. No enemy encountered to prevent any attempt were sent to W. bank of	
		0335hrs	attacking coys (A,C,+D) moved into position representing 400× H. guns SELLE (rifle open order)	
		0449hrs	Enemy suddenly opened fire on ST SOUPLET + positions opposite, including O.C. (Capt NUTTING)	Enemy heavy machine B.coy had some 20 casualties

WAR DIARY or INTELLIGENCE SUMMARY

Army Form C. 2118.

Page 14

Place	Date	Hour	Summary of Events and Information	Remarks and references to Appendices
	17	0520hrs	Batt. advanced to the attack. Crossed the ridge SELLE & PUCKBAKER ridge & reached objective at 0840 hrs. Casualties fairly heavy. There was a thick mist until 0930 hrs. Owing to MG MR leaving coys late in takeing TRENCHES spurs (about 11 casualties) Bt. on left witnesses a slight Rear un getting TRENCH DR HANKES spurs (Ammunition was getting low), At this time leaving emp in Q29 and Q28 to the 1st WILTS Regt. & went further (Montyeline)	
	18	0530hrs	Batts moves forward to the 7 WILTS who attacked through MAZUEL. Batt. B was to keep liaison between WILTS & Americans on Right. Liason posts were established at 3 points (1) R13.c.9.0. (2) R19.a.2.8.3) R24.c.8.8 surrounds of Batts Hug in front – Q.23.7.6.9. – Q.17.a.2.8.	
	19	1900hrs	Batt was withdrawn to Q.19 centre. (VIDE DETAILED ACCOUNT ATTACHED).	

Casualties Officer killed 3 Officers wounded 1 DR Rank 950R wounded 13 " – (at duty)

Prisoners 5 q OR.

M Gs Captured 40 grenader werfer 12. 1 Trench 2 MGs (at duty) 1 D.R returned

Army Form C. 2118.

WAR DIARY
or
INTELLIGENCE SUMMARY.
(Erase heading not required.)

Page 15

Instructions regarding War Diaries and Intelligence Summaries are contained in F. S. Regs., Part II. and the Staff Manual respectively. Title pages will be prepared in manuscript.

Place	Date	Hour	Summary of Events and Information	Remarks and references to Appendices
AVELU	19th	12.30am	Batt. moved (marched) from O I Q centre to AVELU billeting for evening at HONNECHY. Tpt. moved from HONNECHY to AVELU.	
	21st		Batt. in billets. Batt. inspected by G.O.C. 151 Bde (Brig.-Genl. SQUDEN) who congratulated Bn. on their good work.	
	22nd		151 Inf. Bde inspected by G.O.C. 50 Div. (Major-Genl. JACKSON) at TROU AUX SOLDATS 2 officers rejoined temporarily left at DIEPPE.	
	24th		Three officers joined from home.	
	26th		Remaining 163 O.Rs joined. 76 were last left with 4/5th Rifle Brigade and have indifferently joined from U.K.	
	27th		Thanks appreciation movement attended by Corps Commander (SIR T. MORLAND) who inspected battalion afterwards & congratulated him on good work.	
MAUROIS	29th		Bn. Moves to billets in MAUROIS	
	30th		Bn. Moves to billets in LE CATEAU. Transport to O.Q.a B.S. Draft 1 officer & 57 O.R. joined from Base Depot Strength of Batt. on October 1st. 47 officers 952 O.R. " " " " 32 " 618 " Draft joined 6 officers 216 O.R. " " 3 officers & 145 O.R. before DIEPPE were shown H strength of Bn.	

Note:

WAR DIARY
or
INTELLIGENCE SUMMARY

Army Form C. 2118.

Pages 6

Honours & Awards

His Majesty the King granted the Military Medal — for gallantry and devotion to duty in the 3rd-4th 5th Bn the undermentioned under authority granted to the undermentioned O.R.s of K. Battalion for conspicuous gallantry & devotion to duty in the 3rd-4th 5th 6th inst.

6245	CSM	SMITH W.H.	Military Medal
R7918	R/	BARKER F	"
A 3579	"	NORCUP J.T.	"
11810	A/Cpl	COLLINS A.T.	"
C 6664	R/	FOSTER A	"
6577	"	REYNOLDS H.	"
8133	Sgt	PILKINGTON J.	"
7180	R/	CONNOR T.	"
8955	L/c	WILSON H.	"
C 12253	"	MONTHORPE G.	"
R 2479	Cpl	FOX W	"
R 2295	Sgt	PIERCE Dcn. F.	"
R10974	Cpl	THACKER C.T.	Military Medal
9449	R/	NICHOLLS R.	"
R15461	"	BARNETT D.W.	"
11229	"	HILL F	"
R2311	L/c	BOREHAM A.N.	"
R10974	"	MIRON G	"
13265	R/	NETTLETON. H.	"
R7941	"	TERZZA H	"
9683	L/c	LLOYD J	"
11317	Sgt	OWENS M.M.T.	Bar to MM.

Tommy McIntyre
Cmdt 4 Bn

Appendix "E"

List of Casualties for the Month of October, 1918.

	Killed.	Wounded.	W & M. Missing.	Died of Wounds.	W. at duty.
Offrs.	5	14	-	-	2
O.R's.	63	249	2	3	6	7

Total Casualties to date:-

Offrs.	11	48	1	8	2
O.R's.	255	940	8	290	14	7

SECRET.

4th. BATTALION, THE KING'S ROYAL RIFLE CORPS.

OPERATION ORDER No. 191.

3rd October

Ref. MONT BREHAIN 1/20,000

(1) The Brigade will attack and capture the high ground PROSPECT HILL and clear the villages of LE CATELET & GOUY of the enemy on the morning of October 3rd.
    This operation is in conjunction with a major operation on our right flank to be carried out by 2nd. Australian Division.

(2) To the 4th. K.R.R.C. is allotted the task of clearing the villages of LE CATELET & GOUY.
    149th. Brigade will co-operate on left flank of Battn. & take the high ground in A.9.a.

(3) Dispositions for Attack.
    The Battalion will attack on a two Company front, each Coy. being on a two platoon front with two platoons in support. Lines of platoons will be in sections of worms.
    D.Coy. on Right, B.Coy. on Left.
    A.Coy. will support each of the front Coys. with 2 platoons (all four platoons being in one line). A.Coy. will move independantly of the barrage and will exercise utmost care in mopping up all dug-outs and machine gun nests which have NOT been dealt with by front line of attack.
    A.Coy. will form up 200yds. behind the rear of leading Coys. C.Coy. will concentrate on tunnel line in A.15.b. as Battn. Reserve and be ready to move at short notice after 6.15 a.m.

(4) Assembly Position.
    A line parallel to light railway line in A.10.b. A.11.c. A.17.b.& 300 yds. WEST of it.
    Boundaries of Battalion.
    RIGHT. Junction of light Railway with LE CATELET TRENCH in A.11.c.
    LEFT. SUNKEN ROAD in A.10.B & C and west edge of village of LE CATELET.
    FINAL OBJECTIVE. HIGH GROUND NORTH of village in A.4.b. & A.5.a & b.

(5) Artillery.
    A barrage will fall along Light Railway on A.10.b. A.11.c. A.17.b. at 0605 hrs. and remain on this line till 0611 hrs. It will then move forward at the rate of 100 yds. in 4 minutes.
    D.& B. Coys. will follow as close to the barrage as possible (50-76 yds. behind.)

(6) ZERO Hour. is 0605 hrs.
(7) Bn. Hd. Qrs. at A.15.b.8.7.
(8) Acknowledge.

Issued at 0005 hrs.

Captain,
The King's Royal Rifle Corps,
Adjutant, 4th. Battalion.

SECRET.

4th. BATTALION, THE KING'S ROYAL RIFLE CORPS.

OPERATION ORDER No.192.   16th. OCTOBER 1918.

Ref.57.B. 1/40,000.

1. **INTENTION.**

     On the morning of October 17th. the 50th. Division will attack on a front Q.28.c.6.4.-LE CATEAU (exclusive).
     (a) <u>First Objective.</u>
          High ground along Road from Q.23 d. running N. to LE CATEAU.
     (b) <u>Second Objective.</u>
          High ground about R.13. central Q.12.b.-Q.6.d.
     (c) <u>Third Objective.</u>
          Capture of BAZUEL Village.

2. **TASK OF BRIGADE.**

     To the 151st. Inf. Brigade is allotted the task of taking the first objective.

3. **BRIGADE FORMATION.**

     The Brigade will attack on a 3 Battalion front.
          (a) 4th. K.R.R.C. on right.
          (b) 1st. K.O.Y.L.I. in centre.
          (c) 6th. R.INNIS.FUS. on left.

4. **BOUNDARIES.**

     The boundaries of the Battalion will be RIGHT, Q.28.c.6.4.- Road junction Q.23.d.8.3. LEFT Q.22.c.4.4.- Q 17.central.

5. **FLANKING UNITS.**
     The 54th. (American) Inf. Brigade on the RIGHT)
     The 66th. Division   "   "   LEFT)
     will attack simultaneously with 50th. Division.

6. **TASK OF BATTALION.**

     The task of the Battalion will be to clear the ground E. of the River between the Battalion Boundaries XXXXXXXXXXXX as given, up to the high ground immediately E of the Road in Q.17.c.& d & Q.23 b.&d. & to consolidate this high ground when won.

7. **BARRAGE.**

     At Zero hour our barrage will fall along the line of the river in Q 28 b& c & Q.22.c. where it will rest for three minutes.
     It will then move forward at the rate of 100 yds. in 3 minutes.

8. **POSITIONS.**

     By 20.00. hrs. to night 16th., Battalion will be in position of readiness about sunken road in QX28X8X Q.27.d.
     By 04.00 hrs. tomorrow 17th., Battalion will be in position of assembly 200 yds. W. of river in Q.28.y.c.

9. **BRIDGES.**

     R.E. bridging parties with duckboard bridges will be assembled one to each of the four leading platoons by 0400 hrs. on 17t on Battalion Assembly ground.

10. **FORMATIONS.**

     As soon as barrage lifts river will be bridged under R.E. arrangements and Battalion will cross and form up on a 200 yds. front. C.Coy. leading D.Coy. in rear of C.Coy. A.Coy. in rear of D.Coy. at approximately 100yds. distance.
     As soon as leading Coy. has crossed the railway & reached the road in Q.28.b., D.Coy. will move to a flank so as to come into line

Operation Order No.192 (cont)

on LEFT of C.Coy.

The formation for advance will then be C.&D.Coys. on a one platoon front each with one platoon each in close support.

A.Coy. will follow at 200 yds. distance with one platoon in support of each of the attacking Coys.

B.Coy. will be in Battalion reserve & will move with Battalion H.Q.

11. COMPASS BEARING FOR ADVANCE.
C.Coy. 70° (Magnetic)
D. " 65° (do.)

12. TOOLS.

All Coys. will carry under Coy. arrangements sufficient supply of tools for consolidation.

13. BATTALION H.Q.
1st. position (until ZERO) house Q.27.d.3.2.
2nd. " (after ZERO) Q.28.d.1.7.
3rd. " (when objective is taken) cutting Q.23.6.0.

14. COMMUNICATIONS.

Every effort will be made by all Coys. to employ lamps for signalling. Brigade visual station will be in Q.13.d. Battalion visual station on railway embankment about Q.22.d.2.0.

15. ADVANCED BRIGADE AMMUNITION DUMP.
Will be at Q 2.7. central.

16. S.A.A.

Battalion pack animals will be concentrated on Northern outskirts of ST.SOUPLET by 0700 hrs. on 17th. inst. Exact location will be notified later.

17. SYNCHRONIZATION.
Watches will be synchronized at Battalion H.Q. at Midnight.

18. ZERO.

ZERO hour will be notified later.

Captain.
The King's Royal Rifle Corps.
Adjutant, 4th. Battalion.

WAR DIARY. OCTOBER. APPENDIX B.

4th Battalion, The King's Royal Rifle Corps.

Casualty Return.

	2/Lt.	Fryer	W.A.	Killed in Action	3.10.18
	"	Mackay	T.F.	"	"
	"	White	W.A.	"	"
	Capt.	Hayhurst France, M.C., G.F.		Wounded	"
	Lt.	Macaulay, M.C., W.J.C.		"	"
	"	Hardy	E.C.H.	"	"
	2/Lt.	Card	J.S.	"	"
	"	Sutton	G.F.S.	"	"
	"	Methven	W.	"	" at duty.
R9434	Cpl	Jones	J.	Killed in Action	"
12259	L/Sgt	Leach	J.	"	"
7046	Sgt	Delaney	J.	"	"
6/477	"	Horsley	G.	"	"
R21462	Rfn	Bennett	G.	"	4.10.18
3940	Cpl	Morris	J.	"	3.10.18
R38563	Rfn	Scannell	J.	"	"
R39978	"	Hyett	F.	"	"
36197	"	Buchanan	M.	"	"
33172	"	Giles	E.	"	"
R9501	"	Kenworthy	J.	"	"
R18691	"	Roser	R.	"	"
R39736	"	Joyce	H.	"	"
R36680	"	Talbot	H.	"	"
C3589	"	Saunders	H.	"	"
R40260	"	Norman	E.	"	"
7983	"	Carey	B.	" "	"
R5131	"	Gill	A.	"	"
R9808	Cpl	Bailey	W.	"	"
R35861	L/C	Young	J.	" "	"
R7375	"	Dunsby	L.	"	"
10258	Rfn	Clarke	E.	"	"
R8824	"	Elvin	J.	"	"
7099	"	Goodman	R.	"	"
13383	"	Hinchie	J.	"	"
R22546	"	Kirkland	P.	"	" "
R23623	"	Lake	F.	"	"
R24100	"	Mulroy	W.	"	"
R36684	"	Oliver	J.	" "	"
R7162	"	Turner	H.	"	"
R10984	L/C	Thorpe	R.	"	"
45508	Rfn	~~Thorpe~~ Jenkins	D.	"	"
R23185	"	Mace	C.	"	"
R22067	"	Pedgrift	W.	"	"
8899	L/C	Keen	J.	"	"
R24613	Rfn	Bailey	A.	"	"
19289	"	Hatchard	F.	" "	"
9925	L/C	Gibson	N.	Died of Wounds.	5.10.18
R29105	Rfn	Bundy	W.	"	7.10.18
A200833	"	Cavey	T.	"	3.10.18
8457	Sgt	Girdler	W.	"	3.10.18
R727	Rfn	Bull	P.	Wound & Missing	3.10.18
R40698	"	Tuck	F.	Missing	"
R10528	L/C	Wardale	L.	"	"
Y126	L/C	Cannon	A.	Wounded & Missing	"
40237	Rfn	Smith	J.	Wounded	3.10.18
R40663	"	Langford	A.	"	"
R8810	"	Coveney	J.	"	"
R6916	"	Furneaux	G.	"	"

1.

45510	Rfn	Beasley	E.	Wounded	3.10.18	at duty.
R21761	"	Climpson	A.	"	"	"
R40903	"	Hobson	J.	"	"	"
R17358	"	Pritchard	C.	"	"	"
10258	"	Fowler	G.	"	"	
8572	Cpl	Wheeler	A.	"	"	
R9655	"	Peach	E.	"	"	
7896	Rfn	Fuller	A.	"	"	
R17830	"	Finn	R.	"	"	
R33468	"	Dowsett	J.	"	"	
A2039	"	Yates	J.	"	"	
3948	"	Bennett	E.	"	"	
241	Sgt	Clarke	W.	"	"	
C4356	L/C	Oldham	W.	"	4.10.18.	
22055	Rfn	Mann	W.	"	3.10.18	
R40238	"	Winterton	F.	"	"	
Y601	"	Evans	H.	"	"	
R7201	"	Atkins	A.	"	"	
R9492	"	Dalby	S.	"	"	
9466	"	Barnes	C.	"	"	
8220	"	Doak	S.	"	"	
R6812	"	Bromsell	B.	"	"	
Y962	"	Mansfield	J.	"	"	
10534	"	Busbridge	G.	" "	"	
R7937	"	Bain	J.	"	"	
R7901	Sgt	Baker	J.	"	"	
R17164	"	Dyke	H.	"	"	
1285	"	Stephenson	W.	"	"	
3512	A/S	Pearson	J.	"	"	
11563	L/C	Hough	H.	"	"	
R19385	"	Bell	S.	"	"	
R32523	Rfn	Belchamber	W.	"	"	
R36834	"	Boot	E.	"	"	
Y1786	"	Browne	J.	"	"	
R20518	"	Claydon	P.	"	"	
R26640	"	Crutchley	E.	"	"	
R35884	"	Dunse	J.	"	"	
R30428	"	Eames	T.	"	"	
11923	"	Edmondson	H.	"	"	
R23112	"	Fisher	A.	"	"	
Y592	"	Franklin	F.	"	"	
R10005	"	Golder	E.	"	"	
R12109	"	Goodwin	F.	"	"	
6/1032	"	Harwood	S.	"	"	
R40019	"	James	P.	"	"	
R24321	"	le Blond	J.	"	"	
R24068	"	Lippett	J.	"	"	
9683	L/C	Lloyd	J.	"	"	
R35905	Rfn	Mc Leod	J.	"	"	
45517	"	Marshall	G.	"	"	
17447	"	Martin	T.H.	"	"	
R23140	"	Noble	G.	"	"	
R7414	"	Park	J.	"	"	
R19369	"	Pitt	F.	"	"	
45518	"	Prescott	J.	"	"	
R22939	"	Rumney	H.	"	"	
R12909	"	Snowley	H.	"	"	
13411	L/C	Warburton	H.	"	"	
C12364	Rfn	Wood	W.	"	"	
A203108	Cpl	Blaney	L.	"	"	
325224	"	Gross	A.	"	"	

R14718	Cpl	Vasey	J.	Wounded.	3.10.18
8283	L/C	Chamberlain	A.	"	"
A1542	"	Spettigue	J.	"	"
R23045	Rfn	Abbott	W.	"	"
R36701	"	Bowden	G.	"	"
R20916	"	Cheeseman	G.	"	"
11348	"	Darlow	W.	"	"
C6920	"	Dowling	T.	"	"
R15865	L/C	Taylor	G.	"	"
R23667	Rfn	Foxall	W.	"	"
12127	"	Pearson	A.	"	"
R9641	"	Robson	J.	"	"
A1422	"	Salmon	A.	"	"
R40012	"	Smith	E.	"	"
R7465	"	Wood	G.	"	" "
5736	"	Woodhead	W.	"	"
45527	"	Woolley	J.	"	"
6900	Sgt	Walker	H.	"	"
R16490	Cpl	Brown	G.	"	"
R23312	"	Davies	P.	"	"
R11893	"	Wheatley	B.	"	"
8955	L/C	Wilson	H.	"	"
12122	"	Tinsley	J.	"	"
6859	"	Thurlby	A.	"	"
6/128	"	Green	C.	"	"
R40663	Rfn	Langford	A.	"	"
5/4692	"	Roman	A.	"	"
8853	"	Utterson	T.	"	"
R11183	"	Viner	H.	"	"
9807	Sig.	Burgess	F.	"	"
R36254	"	Gosling	A.	"	"
R12426	Rfn	Preston	A.	"	" "
11024	"	Calnan	E.	"	"
R19770	"	Armitage	S.	"	"
5/3374	"	Dodd	E.	"	"
R23015	"	Garnham	H.	"	"
R23760	"	James	J.	"	"
R11617	"	Gallagher	J.	"	"
R39485	"	Holdsworth	F.	"	"
R6121	"	Buckle	C.	"	"
A1591	"	Fallshaw	G.	"	"
12269	"	Head	T.	"	"
A2288	"	Ashton	C.	"	"
R13565	"	Drew	G.	"	"
11673	"	Patey	H.	"	"
R36636	"	Carder	W.	" (Gas)	5.10.18
10502	Sgt	Burridge	S.	" "	"
7714	L/S	Jones	E.	" "	6.10.18
R22548	Cpl	Kilgour	S.	" "	"
10770	Cpl	Brettell	G.	Wounded	9.10.18
45515	Rfn	Bonner	E.	" (Gas)	"
R12810	L/C	Cook	T.	Wounded	"
R26329	Rfn	Ward	H.	"	"
R23024	"	Woodford	W.	"	"
R32757	"	Gould	M.	"	"
R40318	"	Prosser	J.	"	"
6/1252	"	Clarke	E.	"	"
R36692	"	Touhey	W.	"	"
R36693	"	Tierney	M.		

	Lieut.	Preece	H.R.	Killed in Action	8.10.18.	
	"	Munnion	C.E.F.	Wounded	"	
	2/Lt.	Corsby	R.E.	"	"	
	Lieut.	Debnam	P.G.C.	"	"	
	2/Lt.	Austin	A.J.	"	"	at duty.
R3319	Cpl	Hart	W.	Killed in Action	6.10.18	
R16054	Rfn	Sheldon	J.	"	"	
R21400	"	Glover	E.	"	"	
R15541	L/C	Harrison	F.	"	"	
10570	"	Bevis	A.	"	"	
8494	Rfn	Carney	W.	"	"	
Y1858	"	Davies	T.	"	"	
R10230	"	Elvin	A.	"	"	
R13341	L/C	Barrier	P.	Died of Wounds	8.10.18	
5/5090	Rfn	Chamberlain	D.	"	"	
R23965	"	Knott	C.	Killed in Action	"	
R23036	"	Quatromini	B.	Wounded	"	
6/993	"	Haysom	F.	"	"	
R16618	"	Parr	J.	"	"	
R9721	"	Skelton	W.	"	"	
R22659	"	Brown	E.	"	"	
R36665	"	Burgess	C.	"	"	
R6709	Cpl	Healey	F.	"	"	
6888	A/Sgt	Peach	H.	"	"	
R11083	L/C	Brettell	S.	"	"	
R13130	"	Miron	G.	"	"	
R35830	Rfn	Shelley	C.	"	"	
R40993	"	Martin	B.	"	" "	
R20215	"	Read	M.	"	"	
8545	"	Samuels	W.	"	"	
8807	"	Powell	G.	"	"	
8997	Rfn	Manvell	W.	"	"	
R32919	"	Levett	H.	"	"	
6/1332	"	Walker	P.	"	"	
11229	"	Hill	F.	"	"	
R39940	"	Dickle	H.	"	"	
R8015	"	Bradley	J.	"	"	
C7208	"	Whitehead	J.	"	"	
5969	CSM	Lee	F.	"	"	
11377	Sgt	Owens	T.	"	"	
8768	L/C	Coxall	J.	"	"	
8708	"	Merrison	F.	"	"	
R19969	"	Walton	G.	"	"	
R28505	Rfn	Glanville	F.	"	"	
R10592	"	Pickering	B.	"	"	at duty.
R25250	"	Bennett	H.	"	"	"
C12021	Cpl	Brown	W.	"	"	"
R22564	Rfn	Watts	W.	"	"	"
R21759	"	Brown	H.	"	"	
45504	"	Clipstone	G.	accidentally wounded	"	

4th. Battalion, The King's Royal Rifle Corps.

Return of Casualties

	Capt.	Antrobus	M.E.	Wounded	17.10.18.
	"	Eden	G.E.	"	"
	"	Nutting M.C.	A.F.	"	"
	Lieut.	Holgate	H.C.F.	"	"
	2/Lt.	Stewart	R.H.A.	"	"
	"	Powys Jones	L.	"	"
	"	Williams	H.I.	Killed	18.10.18.
B9493	L/Cpl.	Buttery	E.	"	"
6/3835	Rfn.	Lovell	A.	"	"
12802	"	Packer	L.	"	"
7172	A/C.S.M.	Wallace	J.	"	"
9600	Sgt.	Parr	G.	"	"
C12592	Rfn.	Stabler	S.	"	"
10375	Cpl.	Maskell	E.	"	"
200552	Rfn.	Lavester	H.	"	"
R 7641	"	Blake	H.	"	"
R12961	"	Bisk	A.	"	"
R22500	"	O'Brien	T.	"	"
9276	"	Westcombe	C.	"	"
R35692	"	Anderson	R.	"	"
9108	L/Cpl.	Ferguson	T.	"	"
Y 1735	Rfn.	Pardoe	L.	"	"
325220	"	Clarke	H.	"	"
6249	C.S.M.	Smith	H.	"	"
11584	L/Cpl.	Rollinson	J.	Wounded	"
4796	"	Rushton	E.	"	"
11607	"	Hussey	E.	"	"
11375	Rfn.	Bennett	W.	"	"
7118	"	Conner	J.	"	"
R40335	"	Delaney	J.	"	"
A200010	"	Gallon	G.	"	"
R10846	"	Gillison	A.	"	"
B24375	"	Halley	A.	"	"
10067	Sig.	Hines	J.	"	"
R 9581	Rfn.	Jacomb	W.	"	"
R40642	"	Malachinger	E.	"	"
R36675	"	Morris	C.	"	"
9276	"	Roberts	J.	"	"
8761	"	Satterlay	W.	"	"
R 3733	"	Southam	A.	"	"
B33477	"	Warren	A.	"	"
11120	"	Thornton	C.	"	"
R 5367	Cpl.	Ling	A.	"	"
Y 794	"	Cassell	B.	"	"
A 1633	"	Morrison		"	"
R32673	Rfn.	Pearce	A.	"	"
B36950	"	Lyons	W.	"	"
R24301	"	Eden	G.	"	"
9373	"	Fenton	C.	"	"
7751	"	Donald	H.	"	"
C 9303	"	Mooley	F.	"	"
R 9506	"	Norgate	H.	"	"
R30916	"	Cole	J.	"	"
R 3441	"	Stainton	E.	"	"
R25524	"	Dromm	J.	"	"
R15182	"	Lull	H.	"	"
R40918	"	Parks	A.	"	"
R40655	"	Lransgrove	E.	"	"
R14463	"	Johnson	A.	"	"
9500	A/C.S.M.	Reed	G.	"	"
R10414	Sgt.	Bonser	A.	"	"
R 7801	Cpl.	Adams	A.	"	"
9186	"	Loddington	G.	"	"

Number	Rank	Name	Initial	Status	Date
R 7204	Cpl.	Jackson	R.	Wounded	18.10.18.
10352	L/C.	Allinson	W.	"	"
Y 1971	"	Delay	E.	"	"
A201706	"	Harman	A.	"	"
R 979	"	Joseph	W.	"	"
B18652	"	Kitchingman	J.	"	"
R25245	Rfn.	Attewell	A.	"	"
R 35200	"	Butcher	J.	"	"
R 9119	"	Brayford	E.	"	"
C12114	"	Barber	G.	"	"
B17565	"	Bartram	L.	"	"
Y 1603	"	Chrich	F.	"	"
4552P	"	Cousins	S.	"	"
R40460	"	Fennell	W.	"	"
R 9436	"	Gibson	A.	"	"
B10140	"	Mudle	L.	"	"
36217	"	Rudden	C.	"	"
9682	"	Smith	C.	"	"
S/5065	"	Smith	G.	"	"
6680	"	Smart	J.	"	"
C 1692	Sig.	Spence	A.	"	"
B39071	Rfn.	Williams	G.	"	17.10.18.
R12234	"	White	J.	"	"
R 7212	"	Wilkinson	A.	"	"
C 2702	L/C.	Brown	A.	"	"
R23472	Rfn.	Hughendon	A.	"	"
B10081	"	Price	J.	"	"
18855	"	Arrowsmith	T.	"	"
R71963	Sig.	LeFevre	J.	"	"
11800	Rfn.	Challis	J.	"	"
R22401	Cpl.	Hiblons	T.	"	"
7627	L/C.	Perry	B.	"	"
R 9910	Rfn.	Humphreys	C.	"	"
9700	"	Halsey	E.	"	"
9597	"	Kedge	H.	"	"
R 7941	"	Torsey	A.	"	"
B39470	"	Stone	E.	"	"
R20442	L/C.	Bradbury	W.	"	18.10.18.
R22425	Rfn.	Drown	A.	"	"
R36669	"	Haskell	T.	"	"
A 3570	"	Horcup	J.	"	"
B17545	"	Pepper	J.	"	"
R 3972	"	Atkins	F.	"	"
R30362	"	Jones	J.	"	"
R35896	"	Flynn	P.	"	"
R 7985	"	Frodsham	A.	"	"
B20466	"	Pooley	F.	"	"
R36620	"	Judd	H.	Injured	"
9908	"	Golder	R.	Wounded	17.10.18.
B19755	"	Evans	W.	Wounded	"
R2612	"	Hicks	T.	Wounded	"
10086	L/C.	Martin	G.	Missing	" (belived killed)
~~C 4570~~	~~Rfn.~~	~~Wilson~~	~~A.~~	~~Gassed~~	"
R 40606	"	Raines	C.	Gassed	"
~~6/263~~	~~"~~	~~Slater~~	~~H.~~		
R19855	"	Everett	J.	"	"
C12530	"	Walker	C.	"	"
12361	"	Smith	D.	"	16.10.18.
R22397	"	Olney	H.	"	16.10.18.
9609	"	Wood	A.	Wounded	17.10.18. (at duty)
R 8910	L/T.	Dorsham	G.	"	"
6/1205	Rfn.	Hardisty	J.		

//50

WAR DIARY. Vol 6

4th Bn. Kings Royal Rifle Corps

November, 1918

Volume — IV. No 12

4KR: The King's Royal Rifle Corps WAR DIARY

NOVEMBER 1918

Vol IV No 12.

Army Form C. 2118.

Place	Date	Hour	Summary of Events and Information	Remarks and references to Appendices
LECATEAU	1/2		In Billets at LECATEAU - Training - mostly in Lewis Gun.	Ref App 57 Apps 1/40,000
	3rd	8h	See special account attached.	
		9h	Battle surplus rejoined from LANDRECIES. 2nd Lt SEYMOUR reported died of wounds received on 8th	
ST REMY CHAUSSÉE		10h	Funeral of Major G.A. TRYON, M.C. & 6 O.R. in the civilian cemetery at ST REMY CHAUSSÉE.	
		11h	Armistice signed 1100 hours.	
		13h	Funeral of 6 O.R. in cemetery at ST REMY CHAUSSÉE. A Funeral service conducted in French was held at DOURLERS for men of the 151st Infantry Brigade. The Divisional Commander (Maj-General JACKSON D.S.O.) was present & spoke to a speech made by the Maire of DOURLERS. The Battalion supplied the firing party.	
		14h	151st Infantry Brigade Memorial Service for all men killed in action since 3rd October, was held at MONCEAU. the names of the dead being read out by the Commanding officers. There was a procession of inhabitants. The Divisional Commander afterwards	

SECRET.

4th Battalion, The King's Royal Rifle Corps.

OPERATION ORDER, No. 193.

Ref. Sheets 57A & 57B. 1/40,000.   2nd November, 1918.

1. (a) 50th Division will attack the enemy at a date and time to be notified later.
   (b) 25th Division will attack on the RIGHT and 18th Division on the LEFT of 50th Division.

TASK OF BRIGADE. 2. When the 149th and 150th Infantry Brigades, in line from RIGHT to LEFT, have captured RED LINE the BRIGADE will pass through them and capture the GREEN LINE.

FRONTAGE & BOUNDARIES. 3. Boundaries, Dividing lines and Objectives are shown on maps supplied to O's C. Coys.

PLAN OF ATTACK. 4. Brigade will attack and capture the GREEN LINE on a two Battalion front with 4th K.R.R.C. and 1st K.O.Y.L.I. in line from RIGHT to LEFT.
6th R.Innis.Fus.(less 1 Coy) will be in Brigade Reserve
One Coy 6th R. Innis. Fusiliers will be under Command of O.C. 4th K.R.R.C. for a specific purpose (vide para below).

ACTION OF BATTALION. 5. (a) On the afternoon of Y day 4th K.R.R.C. will assemble about LE FAYT FARM.
(b) On Z day at Zero plus 2 hrs 1st K.O.Y.L.I. and 4thK.R.R.C plus one Coy 6th R.Innis Fus. will move to the line of the railway in G.10.a & G.4.c. near DRILL GROUND CORNER. The Coy 6th R. Innis Fusrs will move independently. 1st K.O.Y.L.I. and 4th K.R.R.C. (1st K.O.Y.L.I. leading) will advance approximately on the line through B.9 cent 10 central, 11 central, 12 central, G.7.central, 8 central, 9 central, which will be taped out by R.E. and marked by notice boards "INFANTRY ROUTE TO DRILL GROUND CORNER".
(c) By ZERO plus 4¼ hours 4th K.R.R.C. will be formed up for for the attack, on RED LINE about track running in a N.E. direction through B25 central from the RIFLE RANGE in G.5.d. & G.6.a.
(d) At ZERO plus 5 hours, the Battalion will advance to capture the GREEN LINE, with main line of advance astride the track running N.E. from RIFLE RANGE through B25 central.
At ZERO plus 5 hours the Coy of the 6th R.Innis Fusrs attached to the 4th K.R.R.C. will move as follows:-
Astride the RAILWAY LINE, through G.12.b. and c. H.1.b & c. B.26.b. &c., B.27 a & b, from a point just NORTH of crater at H.7.a.2.8. and make good the railway up to GREEN LINE.
This Coy will establish posts about the RAILWAY as follows:-
No. 1 Post H.7.a.2.8. to cover canal crossing in H.7.b.
No. 2 Post H.2.a.1.9.
No. 3 Post in B.27.a. to cover Canal crossing at B.27.d.1.8.

FORMATION FOR ATTACK. 6. (a) B Coy. will act as ADVANCED GUARD.
(b) A & C Coys will form MAIN BODY, moving in close artillery formation on RIGHT & LEFT of road respectively.
(c) D Coy. will move along road 500 yds behind the main body and will act as escort to section of Field Guns allotted to Battalion.

4th Battalion, The King's Royal Rifle Corps.

Casualty Return.

	Major	Tryon, M.C.	G.A.	Killed in Action	7.11.18.
	2/Lieut.	Seymour	H.	Died of wounds	9.11.18.
	Lieut.	Hayward M.M.F.	E.G.	Wounded	7.11.18.
	"	Bennett	H.S.	"	4.11.18.
	2/Lt.	Warren	F.	"	"
	"	Austin	A.J.	"	7.11.18.
	"	Schofield	F.G.	"	4.11.18: (at duty
		S			
	Capt.	Edmond	J.J.L.(R.A.M.C.)	"	7.11.18.
8778	Sgt.	Lucas	G.	Killed in action	7.11.18.
R 9602	L/C	Wright	E.	" "	4.11.18.
R 2478	Cpl.	Fox	W.	" "	7.11.18.
R18725	L/C	Watson	A.	" "	"
R 5976	"	Hutchings	H.	"	
R2479	Cpl	Fox, M.M.	W.	"	"
R18725	L/Cpl	Watson	A.	"	"
325222	Rfn	Hayward	C.	"	"
R36698	"	Johnston	E.	"	"
R23657	"	Lambell	E.	"	4.11.18
R14645	Rfn	Pitcher	W.	"	7.11.18
59659	"	Goch	G.	"	4.11.18
47707	"	Wright	R.	"	"
56243	"	Passingham	W.	"	"
	"	Crook	H.	Wounded	9.11.18
R31834	"	Gibson	J.	Killed	7.11.18
7723	"	Phillips	T.	"	"
56247	"	Bowe	F.	"	"
Y1007	"	West	F.	"	"
12328	"	Ashworth	F.	"	"
R23747	"	Abbott	W.		
R23045	"	Wakefield	R.	Died of Wounds	5.11.18
45513	"	Wheat	J.	"	6.11.18
10497	L/C	Hoile	A.	"	7.11.18
10769	Rfn	Cuthbertson	F.	Killed in Action	"
12151	Cpl	Thacker, M.M.,	T.	Wounded	" Died of Wounds 8/18
R10974	Sgt	Blight	H.	"	"
13621	"	Johnson	H.	"	4.11.18
10157	Cpl	Carrington	W.	"	7.11.18
56194	"	Spurin	F.	"	"
56196	L/C	Clarke	F.	"	"
6/5085	"	Elliman	J.	"	"
A1806	"	Margetts	E.	" "	
6/9912	"	Pumfrey	F.	"	"
11460	"	White	R.	"	"
56206	Rfn	Atkinson	T.	"	"
47792	"	Burns	H.	"	"
21129	"	Brigham	J.	"	"
7928	"	Connington	A.	"	"
46151	"	Church	P.	"	"
56211	"	Clifton	T.	"	Died of wounds 9/18
R26334	"	Corby	T.	"	4.11.18
R11793	"	Gamlin	W.	"	7.11.18
47153	"	Hobson	J.	"	"
R40903	"	Judd	J.	"	"
11396	"	Pickthorne	A.	"	9.11.18
A1787	"	Potter	F.		
47048					

R9803	Rfn.	Boswell	A.	Wounded.	4.11.18.
33479	"	Chaplin	H.	"	7.11.18.
8147	"	Gunn	W.	"	4.11.18.
33678	"	Guthrie	W.	"	7.11.18.
56225	"	Hyde	E.	"	"
56232	"	Hatton	J.	"	
Y189	"	Holmes	J.	"	4.11.18.
Y1102	"	Jones	J.	"	"
56246	"	Puplett	S.	"	7.11.18.
56249	"	Patrick	C.	"	4.11.18.
10977	"	Pardoe	H.	"	"
36686	"	Phillips	F.	"	8.11.18.
R10167	"	Riley	J.	"	7.11.18.
C12810	Sig.	Russom	W.	"	4.11.18.
21436	Rfn.	Rugg	J.	"	7.11.18.
R17369	"	Simmonds	G.	"	"
R9729	"	Scarisbrick	R.	"	4.11.18.
45525	"	Sutton	G.	"	7.11.18.
R10161	"	Taylor	A.	"	"
56261	"	Tye	C.	"	"
R22569	"	Watts	W.	"	"
Y386	Sgr.	Ward	W.	"	4.11.18.
9302	Rfn.	Neville	B.	"	7.11.18.
56270	"	Skeels	W.	"	" (at duty)
56256	"	Sharp	D.	"	" (at duty)
45502	"	Beebe	J.	"	"
23154	"	Lee	R.	"	"
R21759	"	Brown	H.	"	"
R9646	L/c.	Leach	S.	"	"
9750	"	Lardner	A.	"	"
R25521	"	Allen	W.	"	"
R23129	"	Robinson	W.	"	"
R19441	"	Palley	F.	"	"
7733	"	Tucker	G.	"	"
5495	"	Goatley	J.	"	8.11.18. Died of Wounds 9/8
R38240	L/c.	Munson	A.	"	"
Y1251	Rfn.	Bachelor	A.	"	"
56244	"	Priddis	W.	"	"
R10258	"	Fowler	G.	"	"
R36851	"	Smith	W.	"	"
56238	"	Miller	R.	"	"
56251	"	Reynolds	F.	"	"
Y157	"	Lord	A.	"	7.11.18. & rejd.10.11.18
Y1148	"	Toogood	A.	"	8.11.18 (at duty)
R21704	"	Allen	W.	"	7.11.18.
45515	"	Benning-	S.	"	"
R11576	L/c.	Gray	J.	"	"
9426	Sgt.	Jackson	J.	"	" Died of Wounds 4/8
8788	L/c.	Bussey	J.	"	"
R7074	Rfn.	Barnes	R.	"	" Died of Wounds 16/8
9631	"	Clarke	S.	"	"
R28545	"	Druty	G.	"	"
13266	"	Smith	J.	"	"
R6659	"	Slade	L.	"	5.11.18.
9657	"	Bowen	H.	"	4.11.18.
32526	"	Griffiths	A.	wounded	"
R22688	"	Hughes	E.	wounded	"
58223	"	Glover	A.	"	7.11.18.
Y257	"	Moyse	J.	"	"
47794	"	Patrick	R.	"	"
9232	"	Taylor	J.	Killed in Action	
23045	"	Abbott	W.	wounded	8.1.18.
56227	"	Harvey	S.	Acc. Wounded	7.11.18.
56272	"	Marshall	A.	Wounded	8.11.18
12035	"	Clark	W.C.		

R40330	Rfn	Cronin	J.		Wounded(Gas) 9.11.18
8139	Rfn	Park	H.		Wounded 7.11.18
R9267	"	Radford	A.		" "
47811	"	Richardson	F.		" "
47084	"	Squires	P.		" "
50325	"	Stimson	H.		" "
47836	"	Storme	G.		" " — Died of Wounds 9/18
12178	"	Tidswell	P.		" 4.11.18 Died of Wounds
R26323	"	Tilbrook	A.		5.11.18
R9639	"	Uttley	J.		" 7.11.18
R21091	"	Wheeler	T.		" " Died of Wounds 9/7/18
46917	"	Williamson	J.		" "
R16453	"	Wells	W.		" "
47810	"	Wilson	G.		" "
46854	"	Warren	J.		" 4.11.18
R21378	"	Keen	T.		" "
60426	"	Edwards	T.		" "
R30437	"	Taylor	J.		" "
C7750	"	Green	W.		" "
56230	"	Hatch	J.		" "
47172	"	Robinson	T.		" "
47020	"	Lewis	T.		" "
R9249	L/C	Denby	A.		" "
56242	Rfn	Percy	L.		" "
56881	"	Davis	E.		" "
R1223	"	Gray	T.		" "
R7353	"	Williamson	T.		" "
47080	"	Gates	W.		" " Died of Wounds
R29027	Cpl	Pond	W.		9.11.1918.
56264	Rfn	Walton	J.		" 5.11.18.
56262	"	Whittington	G.		" "
R6617	"	Harris	H.		" 7.11.18.
56231	"	Harrington	T.		" "
R16961	"	Lloyd	R.		" "
R5861	"	Warren	E.		" "
R2906	"	Viney	F.		" "
R12840	"	Binns	J.		" 8.11.18.
6/1302	"	Hudson	A.		" "
40332	"	Mayers	W.		" "
56197	Cpl.	Merrett	G.		" "
56267	Rfn.	Watson	A.		" "
R40437	"	Dobson	A.		" "
R9932	"	Willcock	J.		" "
6/1019	"	Currey	F.		" "
R9663	"	Vernon	W.		" "
R23574	"	Ingle	J.		" "
47601	"	Chapman	J.		" "
47775	"	Coulson	S.		" " — Died of Wounds 13/11/18
56209	"	Baker	J.		" "
56214	"	Burgess	A.		" "
47805	"	Blazey	H.		" "
47082	"	Thomson	J.		" "
10573	Sgt.	Riley	F.		" "
56239	Rfn.	McWhinney	T.		" 7.11.18. D of W 9/11/18
56220		Ficken	H.		" " rejnd. 10.11.18.
45512	Rfn.	Welch	R.		" "
8520	A/C.S.M.	Turner	A.		" "
R22653	L/c.	Gilkes	E.		" 8.11.18.
11562	Rfn.	Aldridge	S.		" "
45520	"	Ashmore	S.		" "
9612	"	Ashton	R.		Missing "
56250	Rfn	Peggs	D.		Wounded "
47807	"	Meek	W.R.		

APPENDIX "B"

TOTAL CASUALTIES for month ended 30th November, 1918.

	Killed.	Wounded.	W & M.	Missing.	Died of Wds.	Wd at duty
Officers	1	4	-	-	1	1
" (R.A.M.C)		1				
Other Ranks	19	132	-	-	20	2

TOTAL CASUALTIES TO DATE:-

	Killed.	Wounded.	W & M.	Missing.	Died of Wds.	Wd at duty
Officers	12	53	1	8	2	3
Other Ranks	274	1072	3	290	34	9

3rd November to 9th November, 1918.

November 3rd. The Battalion moved in marching order from LE CATEAU to point L.9.b.4.6. camping for the night in an orchard 600 yards S.W. of BOUSIES. Battalion H.Q. was established in a house in BOUSIES.

The Battle Surplus was left in LE CATEAU & the transport moved up to Point L.9c.b.4.6.

The Fighting portion of the Battalion consisted of 17 Officers & 303 Other Ranks. "A" Company & "B" Company were organised in three platoons each whilst "C" & "D" Companies were organised in 2 platoons each.

The weather, which was fine in the morning, changed for the worse about 17.00 hrs and it rained most of the night. Trench shelters were drawn, but not until 18.30 hrs, & most of the men got very wet. About 21.30 hrs the Divisional Commander (Major General JACKSON) visited Battalion H.Q. & later the D.C.C. 151st Infantry Brigade (Brig: General SUGDEN) also visited the Battalion.

Zero hour was fixed at 06.15 hrs and notified to the Battalion at 19.30 hrs. Rations were very late reaching the Battalion owing to a breakdown on the railway; they did not arrive until 02.30 hrs on morning of 4th.

November 4th. The Battalion marched from bivouac ground at 06.45 hrs in Fighting Order, packs being dumped under a guard at the Cross Roads in L.9.b. The Commanding Officer rode ahead with the L.C.C. & the Battalion followed along the tape marked track running through L.10,11,12, central and on due E.

At about 07.00 hrs an order was received from Brigade that Battalion was not to move further than Pt C.3.d.5.5. on the RAU DE L'HIRONDELLE. On arrival at this point about 11.30 hrs verbal orders were received for the Battalion to advance to the attack up the LAIE DE MONT CARMEL as far as GREEN LINE running through Pts E.8.d.9.0., E.14.c.0.6.; & L.16.c.3.8.; where it was to consolidate in depth. The 2/A.C.Y.L.I. were to advance simultaneously up the ROUTE DE FONTAINE & the 6/ R.I.F. up the ROUTE DE LANDRECIES. Formation adopted by the Battalion:- "B" Company, under Capt. G.H. WELLS, M.C., Advanced Guard, "A" Company, under Capt. H.L. LULLER, Right Flank Guard, remainder Main Body in following order:- " C" Company, under Capt. E.J. TRYTER, M.C., "D" Company under 2/Lieut W. METHVEN, "H.Q" Company under Lieut. L.G. BURGOYNE.

Contact was obtained with the enemy about Pt. A.29.c.4.4. hostile machine gun posts & snipers firing from wood in A.30.a. A number of casualties were incurred in dislodging the enemy from this position. Considerable resistance was received from an armoured car moving along the ROUTE DE LANDRECIES. From this point onwards more or less continuous touch was maintained with the enemy who appeared to be fighting a rear guard action with Cavalry Machine Gunners. The ground afforded ample cover for this procedure & made a rapid advance difficult. It was not until 15.45 that our Advanced Guard reached the E. edge of Wood in L.19.b. On debouching from the wood it was found that the enemy was making a determined stand on the high ground in L.14.c. the Advanced Guard coming under heavy M.G. fire. It was found impossible to get forward under the fire so "D" Company were ordered to work round on our right flank, through wood in L.20.c. and to dislodge the enemy by working up the ridge on his flank. This manoeuvre was entirely successful and the crest of the ridge was captured just as dusk was falling

at about 12.00 hrs. Orders were received from 151 Inf. Bde.
to move over to our right and consolidate on GREEN LINE through
pts L.21.v.25,80. to L.21.d.80.45. (inclu) after capture.

It was now too late to attempt the side stepping involved in
this order & it was decided to consolidate on the ridge then
held & touch was obtained with 1/A.C.Y.L.I. on left and
6/R.I.R. on right. "B" & "D" Companies established themselves
in an old German trench on the reverse slope just below the
crest. "E" Company were in support 200 yards behind and "A"
Company in reserve at Pt. L.19.d.5.6. where Battalion H.Q. was
also established. At about 23.00 hrs by 151 Brigade orders
were received that the Battalion would attack at 06.30 hrs.
- objectives N. Bank of SAMBRE RIV. from Pt. L.15.c.5.6.
to L.24.c.0.4. A Battalion of E. SURREY REGT (18th Div:) were
to attack on our left & the 6/R.I.R. on our right. In order
to allow the 6/R.I.R. to assemble on a front more favourable
to their line of advance "A" Coy, 4/K.R.R.C. relieved 2
Companies 6/R.I.R. holding line from Pt. L.20.b.0.4. to
L.20.d.4.1. (incl.) at about 01.30 hrs.

Enemy shelled line intermittently throughout the night
"A" Company suffering some casualties; there were also
occasional bursts of harrassing M.G. fire.

Casualties throughout the day's fighting were 3 Officers
& 30 Other Ranks (approximately), the Officers wounded
being Lieut. H.C. LENNETT, 2/Lieut. F. WARREN, & 2/Lt. B.G.
SCHOFIELD. *During the advance A. Coy. captured an 8" howitzer.*

After consolidation telephonic communications were
established between Battalion H.Q., Brigade H.Q., and
Companies in the line.

November 5.   The Battalion advanced to the attack at 06.30 hrs.
"A" Company & "B" Company in front line from right to left
"D" Company in support and "C" Company in reserve. Very
little resistance was offered by the enemy the front line
reaching Pt. L.21.b.5.5. before contact was established.
The ground over which the Battalion advanced was shelled but
few casualties were sustained. The Battalion was in position
on its objective by 08.30 hrs & Headquarters established in
railway cutting at point L.23.a.7.3. & touch obtained with
Battalion on right & left.
"A" Coy & "B" Coy held river bank with a series of L.G. posts.
The remainder of their Companies were withdrawn to wood in
L.23 b & d. "D" Company remained in support in wood in L.23 a.
b. & d. "C" Company in reserve in wood in L.22 b. A post of
1 N.C.O. & 6 Other Ranks was established at Lock in L.18.d.
The weather was extremely bad - raining all day and the
following night.

The casualties sustained during the day operations were
slight.

During the night 2/Lt. FULLER took out a patrol to
reconnoitre the GRANDE HELPE EAU in G.19 and returned with
valuable information required by higher authority.

Telephonic communication was maintained with Brigade H.Q.

November 6.   Orders were received for 151 Inf. Bde to concentrate in
HATCHETTE FARM area, 4/K.R.R.C. in L.22.c by 09.30 hrs. Camp
was pitched at Pt. L.22.c.5.5. trench shelters being erected
for the men. The cookers and water carts arrived at 11.15
hours. Orders were received at 11.00 hrs for 151 Inf. Bde
to concentrate at HATCHETTE FARM as soon as possible. In order
to allow the men to have the hot soup which the cookers brought
the Battalion did not parade until 12.00 hrs when it marched
to Assembly Point arriving there 12.40 hrs. Orders were then
received for Brigade to march to billets in NOYELLES, head

of Brigade Column to cross Bridge in D.27.a. at 13.30 hrs. The Battalion moved at 13.40 which just allowed time for the men to get tea off the cookers which remained at HATCHETTE FARM. The Battalion arrived N.T.E. NOYELLES about 16.00 hrs where it was put into quite good billets for the night. Fires were got going & socks and boots dried as far as possible. At 21.00 hrs orders were received for the Brigade to march at 06.00 hrs for St. REMY CHAUSSEE where it was to pass through 152 Inf. Bde & advance to the attack. Intermediate objective road from Cross Roads in D.11 c. (excl) to Pt. D.17.a.9.0. Final objective MAUBEGE - AVESNES road Pt. E.7.b.6.1. (stream inclusive) to E.13.d.7.6. (BRASSERIE incl.). The 6/R.I.F. were to operate on the right of the Battalion & a Brigade of 98th Divn. on left.

Route to be followed by Battalion Pt. D.13.C.9.7. - POT DE VIN - Cross Roads in D.11.c. - Wood in D. 12.c. & S. of DOURLERS to objective.

Route to be followed by 6/R.I.F. Pt. D.13.c.9.7. - St. AUBIN- S. of DOURLERS to objective.

November 7.   Rations did not come up before the Battalion left NOYELLES, a rum issue only being made. Orders were issued for the consumption of emergency rations.

The Battalion marched at 06.00 hrs - LEVAL - MONCEAU - St REMY CHAUSSEE arriving the last named place at 08.40 hrs. The Advanced Guard (D. Company under command of 2/Lt. MATTHEWS) left fork roads at D.13.c.9.7. at 08.50 hrs. the remainder of the Battalion keeping to the road in the following order - "C" Company, "A" Company, "B" Company, & "H.Q." Company. The road was subjected to slight shelling but no casualties were incurred between ST. REMY CHAUSSEE & POT-DE-VIN. On arrival at latter place it was discovered that 19 th Inf. Bde had already established an Advanced Brigade Hd Qrs there From this source information was obtained that a Battalion of 19th Brigade was pushing through the wood on N. side of road running through D.10. a. & b. The Battalion therefore pushed on as quickly as possible into and through the wood on the S. side of the road. A number of casualties from shell fire were sustained between POT-DE- VINne D.10.Central.

On debouching from the wood into the orchards in D.10.d. the Advanced Guard came under fairly heavy M.G. fire from the road in D.11.c. & searching fire from points further back. The advanced Guard was temporarily held up about 400 yards short of the road. The Commanding Officer (Major G.A. TRYON, M.C.) went forward to the Advanced Guard to review the situation and was unfortunately shot through the head whilst conferring with O.C. "D" Company. "C" Company was then sent to make a flanking movement on Right through D.18.b. & D.17.a. and "A" Company a similar movement on left & Capt. M.L. FULLER sent for to take command of the Battalion. The flanking movement was successful in dislodging the enemy M.G's and that intermediate objective was captured at 10.15 hrs. The Brigade O.C. stated that no further advance would be made until orders were sent to Battalions to do so, mounted orderlies being used for communication. The position was therefore consolidated "C" Company & "A" Company in the front line from right to left, touch being obtained with 6/R.I.F. on right. "B" & "D" Coys were in support & reserve at Pts D.17.d.7.3. & D.10.d.5.2. respectively. The position was shelled intermittently for the first half hour but few casualties were sustained.
"D" Company lost a number of men in attacking the position & "C" Company also sustained fairly heavy casualties.

At 13.00 hrs orders were received from 151 Inf. Bde for the Battalion to advance to the final objective. Formation adopted "A" Company (under 2/Lt. AUSTIN) Advanced Guard, "C" Company in support followed by "D" and "B" Companies in reserve. Distances

of 300 yards to 400 yards were maintained between Companies.
Line of advance followed 200 yards N. of & parallel to road running through 9.11.c & D. as far as wood in D.12.c. thence due E to objective. The Advanced Guard came under M.G. & snipers fire on reaching high ground at point D.11.c.3.7. & had difficulty in advancing further than Pt. D.11.d.5.5. Both "A" Coy & "C" Coy sustained a number of casualties from the fire. An enemy M.G. was located in house at Point D.11.d.8.5.C. & 2 Platoons of "B" Company were sent to work round the position on the S. side of the road, whereupon the enemy withdrew. On reaching the wood in D.12.c. it was discovered to be very dense with thick undergrowth so the advance was continued round the Northern boundary of the wood as far as Pt. D.12.c.9.4. which point was reached at 14.40 hrs. Here the enemy M.G. fire increased considerably in intensity & enemy trench mortar fire was opened on the buildings around this point. From here onwards enemy resistance stiffened; the country became very close the hedges being high & thick & only passable through narrow gaps which was liable to cause undue bunching & delay. By this time "A" Company as Advanced Guard had become considerably weakened by casualties and "C" Company was therefore pushed through them "A" Company following in close support. An effort was made to obtain communication with 6/R.I.F. but owing to the fact that the Village of DOURLERS was in between uncleared & to the large interval separating the lines of advance of the two units at this point it was unsuccessful.

Point E.7.d.c.7 was reached by Advanced Guard after a slow advance maintained under continuous M.G. fire at 15.40 hrs. Here it seemed the enemy intended putting up a determined resistance as very intense M.G. fire was opened from the line of the MAUBEUGE - AVESNES road & a field gun commenced firing over open sights from approximately Pt. E.7.d.5.5. inflicting some casualties on the Reserve Company & H.Q. Company. Enemy M.G. fire was also opened from the flanks showing that flanking Units were not in line with the Battalion. It was now very misty & rapidly growing dark. An effort was made by "C" Company reinforced by "A" Company to push forward with "D" Company working on right flank but enemy fire was too intense and heavy casualties were sustained amounting to about 50% of the day's fighting.

At 1900 hrs (approximately) it had grown so dark that it was decided to consolidate having in view the fact that communication was not obtained with flanking units. The position the Battalion was then in was most unsuitable for consolidation being on lower ground than the line of MAUBEUGE - AVESNES road & the country much intersected by thick hedges; it was therefore decided to withdraw to a more suitable position and one from which a better kick off could be obtained the following morning. The withdrawal was methodically carried out, it now being too dark and misty for the enemy to observe our movements though the M.G. fire continued throughout the withdrawal. "C" Company formed the rear Guard and covered the withdrawal. The first line to which withdrawal was made was the line of the road running through E.7.a. & D.12.d. This was found unsuitable for consolidation owing to lack of field of fire, difficulty of communication from front to rear & bend in road in centre of line at Cross Roads in D.12.d. it was therefore decided to withdraw on to road running through D.12.a & b. & final consolidation was made here. A, C & B Coys in front line from right to left & D. Company in reserve, the line extending from DOURLERS - MONT DOURLERS ROAD on the right to Pt D.12.a.7.c. on the left.

Touch was obtained with C. Coy of 1/K.O.Y.L.I. on the DOURLERS - MONT DOURLERS ROAD but no connection could be found with unit on the left though patrols were sent a considerable distance up the road through D.12.a. Battalion H.Q. was established at Point D.12.c.5.8. Officer casualties for the day's (igh ting Major G.A. TRYON, M.C., killed. 2/Lt. SEYMOUR wounded (since died of wounds) 2/Lt. AUSTIN wounded, & Capt. J.J.L. EDMUND (R.A.M.C) wounded. Approximately 80 Other Ranks.

About 15 stretcher cases were collected in house at D.12.c.8.4.2 it was not until midnight that these were cleared. The inhabitants of the house were unsparing in their labours to alleviate the sufferings of the wounded and were of the greatest assistance to the staff of the R.A.P.

At 17.30 hrs H.Q. Section of M.G. Coy reported to the Battalion & its guns were utilised to protect flanks of the front line.

During the night 2 battalions of the Royal Welsh Fusiliers passed through our line prior to concentrating in road in E.1.d. & E.7.a. for an attack which was to be launched about 15.00 hrs.

November 8. At 06.30 hrs orders were received from 151 Inf. Bde for the advance to continue to the final objective (MAUBEUGE – AVESNES ROAD) at 07.30 hrs & orders were issued accordingly.

"B" Company (under command of Capt. G.R. WELLS, M.C.) to form advanced guard "D" Company (under command of 2/Lt. W. METHVEN) and "C" Company (under command of Capt. R.J. TRUTER, M.C.) in close support, with "A" Company (under command of 2/Lt. FULLER) in reserve. Line of advance to be by road from Point D.12.c.0.3. to Cross Roads at D.12.d.2.6. thence due E. to objective. The Battalion was to take and consolidate objective between following bounds Point E.7.b.5.2. (inclusive) & E.7.d.6.2. (inclusive).

At about 05.30 hrs Lt. Col BRADY J.L., D.S.O., arrived at Battalion H.Q. and took over command from Capt. M.L. FULLER.

The attack was launched according to plan at 07.30 hrs. Rate of progress was not rapid owing to enemy M.G. fire from front & right of flank. Steady progress, however, was made & position captured by 09.30 hrs. Fairly heavy casualties were incurred during the advance and the position was subjected to heavy shelling after capture from which further casualties resulted during consolidation.

Consolidation was as follows:- "B", "C" & "D" Companies in front line from right to left on MAUBEUGE – AVESNES ROAD within allotted boundaries. Lewis Gun posts were pushed out short distances on E. side of road. Communication was established with Units on both flanks. Battalion Headquarters was situated at Pt.D.12.d.8.7.

A Section of Machine Gunners, under Lt. GREAVES, 50th M.G.C rendered valuable assistance both during the advance and after consolidation by giving accurate overhead covering fire from a position at D.12.d.2.8. first on to the MAUBEUGE – AVESNES road & later on to the high ground 500 yards E. of the main road.

DOBBIN At about 22.30 hrs the Battalion was relieved by 2nd Royal Fusiliers and marched back to billets in St. REMY CHEMOSSEE.

To tal casualties incurred during the fighting from 4th November to 8th November (both inclusive) 6 Officers & 173 O.R's.

The greatest difficulty with which the Battalion had to contend was the extreme fatigue of the men on 7th & 8th as a result of the rapid advances and great distance covered.

WAR DIARY or INTELLIGENCE SUMMARY

Army Form C. 2118.

Page 2.

Place	Date	Hour	Summary of Events and Information	Remarks and references to Appendices
STRENY CHAUSSEE	NOVEMBER 15.		Bn moved to LA SOUFFRANCE FARM in the mud to TOT DE VIN.	(EUN)
	16.		Draft of 3 officers & 90 joined. The following were taken on appeared in D.R.O's. CAPT G H HAYHURST-FRANCE MC — Bn to MC. 2Lt G E S SUTTON MC. Lieut C E F MUNNION — MC. 1 Lt W METHEN — MC. 7172 Sgt WALLACE (since killed in action) — DCM. 8623 Sgt DUCKWORTH — DCM 6888 Cpl LEACH. DCM	(EUN)
	18.		Major J GROOMBRIDGE MC joined Batt⁻. Capt M E ANTROBUS from Hospital returned.	(EUN)
	19.		A & C Coys moved to DOMPIERRE for salvage work in DOMPIERRE area. Batt⁻ working parties on to releived at DOMPIERRE station. Ammunition dump	(EUN)
	20. 21. 22.			
	23.			(EUN)
	24. 25.		Lieut G E A P GAMES TSO given that men temporary commanding 13. lecture to JB Battn proceeded to U.K. to Sphere Leave. Relieve in there trenches Entries in reference sheets. was given attached to see of 14 MMG mounted work up for positions during operations 4th – 7th Appendix. Company in effects much to DOMPIERRE very good from tracing (EUN) reconnection where attachments for Bricks Coy —	(EUN)
	26.			
	30.		in no officer minu on 13 Nov: 32: 42: 6.18 OR. STRENGTH of B⁻ 533 JOHNSON 19 officers 129 OR.	

WR 7

WAR DIARY.

4th Bn. Kings Royal Rifle Corps

December 1918.

Vol IV

4th Bn THE KING'S ROYAL RIFLE CORPS WAR DIARY or INTELLIGENCE SUMMARY.

DECEMBER 1918 Vol. II No. 13

Army Form C. 2118.

Place	Date	Hour	Summary of Events and Information	Remarks and references to Appendices
DOMPIERRE	1		The Educational Classes were got into working order. About 80 men attending classes in French, English, Arithmetic. About 20 men were attached to the various battalion shops for instruction.	Ref. maps F7/11 F.B. Yronne 57 S/Sheet 1/40,000
	2		Lt. E.N. WILKINS joined from the base.	
	3		A.M. The King passed through the 50th Divisional Area. He halted for a short time at X roads in J 2A, where the infantry battalions were lining the roads. The following honours rewards affected in 50th Nov. R.O. 441 3 Lt (A/Capt.) G.K. WELLS, M.C. the D.S.O. Lt H.G.N. DAVIES (4/KRR) the M.C. Lt H.S. BENNETT the M.C. R.4726 Sgt. KYMER the D.C.M. 8772 Sgt. BUCKLEY the D.C.M.	
	4		2 Lt SCHOFIELD & 2 Lt BUTLER left battalion to 4th Area Commandants at BERMERIES & SAUZOAR respectively.	
	5		The battalion moved from DOMPIERRE to AMFROIPRET where it was billetted in a very scattered area. The division between companies much hindered the Educational Scheme but recreational training was continued & a lot of football was played. Battalion Headquarters was situated at No 42.14.	
	8		Companies moved to new billets in BAVISIAUX	

4th Battn. THE KING'S ROYAL RIFLE CORPS. WAR DIARY

INTELLIGENCE SUMMARY

Army Form C. 2118.

DECEMBER 1918

Place	Date	Hour	Summary of Events and Information	Remarks and references to Appendices
AMFROIPRET	11		A boxing competition was held at Battalion Headquarters. There were about 30 competitors took part & some keen boxing was seen.	
	12		A/Major Parkes M.C. from 1/5 Bn was joined as second in Command.	
	14		The following Strewn Prosouls appeared in 50th Divl. R.O. wo 57. Capt. J.J.B. EDMOND. R.A.M.C. the M.C. LIEUT. W.M.W. COLLINS (DORSET REGT.) the M.C. 2LT. E.W. FULLER the M.C.	
	17		The Battalion moved into excellent billets at LA LONGUEVILLE.	
	18		2LT. THEAK left battalion to the 151ST Inf. Brs. Cashier Office. Educational classes recommenced, about 80 men attending.	
	19		A draft of 19 O.R's joined from base.	
	21		LT. COL. J.B. BRADY rejoined Battalion. LT. COL. A.A. SOAMES, who had been in command during his absence, went to 53rd Divl. Headquarters.	
	24		Arieu left battalion shortly had to England. 2LT. WOODWARD h. UK on leave(?) Successful Battalion Sports were held the R.F.C. 1st & 2nd Inf. Bde attached.	
	26		Education Scheme was reorganized: 137 men started attending classes. A certain amount of work to Enlighten men Command & proper roads.	
	30			

WAR DIARY

4TH BN. KING'S ROYAL RIFLE CORPS

JANUARY 1919

Vol. 5   No. 2

Vol 8

4th Bn The King's Royal Rifle Corps WAR DIARY   JANUARY 1919

INTELLIGENCE SUMMARY.   VOL I.   No 2.

Place	Date	Hour	Summary of Events and Information	Remarks and references to Appendices
LALONGUEVILLE	1st	3ᵖ	Training ½ hour in the morning — Educational classes in French, English, Arithmetic & afternoon attended to by the Battalion shops. (EMcarp)	R/f Street 51 /19003.
	4th		Matches in Boxing. The British Columbia team won the heavy and light heavy weights — Also were runners up in the Bantamweights (ELM)	
	5th		There probably will be some commands formed to the UK. (EM)	
	15th		A lecture on "The British Columbia train we attended "Reasons of Ar. Ronald Guernar B.A. — (EM)	
	2nd		Future were country run in the afternoon. (BR)	
	17th		Lecture on GAMES v30 winners of T.S. Trainy H80. (ELD)	
	18th		Area Attendance of T.S. Trainy H80. The B.C. won the Heavy weight at Finals of Corps Boxing — (ELM)	
	16-18		2nd in Bantam weight.	
	20th		The Officers of the B3n furnished a mimic where in "manufacturing" was attended to by Capt Moore. (ELM)	

WAR DIARY
or
INTELLIGENCE SUMMARY.

Army Form C. 2118.

Place	Date	Hour	Summary of Events and Information	Remarks and references to Appendices
	28.3.19		Agra desert has thawed first. Training continued as laid down. (HLN)	
			Salvage area was cleared by further working parties which were extended to last furnace. Returned was the war material.	
			Investigation. The firing was undertaken on munition 23 Ry. so many bays than 2 years to secure one detachment (HLN)	
			Sheigh 1.1.19. 44 officers 560 OR.	
			" 31.1.19. 42 " 610 "	
	31.1.19			

Lawson Miller
Comdt 4 Bn

aid Soames

CONFIDENTIAL.

WAR DIARY.

4th Bn. THE KINGS ROYAL RIFLE CORPS.

1st to 28th FEBRUARY, 1919.

VOLUME V. No 3.

4th Bn. THE KING'S ROYAL RIFLE CORPS   WAR DIARY   Army Form C. 2118.
                                           or
Instructions regarding War Diaries and Intelligence   INTELLIGENCE SUMMARY.   FEBRUARY 1919
Summaries are contained in F. S. Regs., Part II.
and the Staff Manual respectively. Title pages   Vol. V. No. 3.
will be prepared in manuscript.
                                        (Erase heading not required.)

Place	Date	Hour	Summary of Events and Information	Remarks and references to Appendices
LA LONGUEVILLE				
	10th		10 Officers and 150 O.R's returned to form the 1st Batt" on the Army of Occupation.	A/M
	14th		The RHINE Draft was inspected by the Divisional Commander (B.Gen. Robinson) and by the Brigade Commander.	A/M A/M A/M
	17th		Warning order received for the Batt" to proceed to JOLIMETZ.	A/M
	21st		Batt" moved from LA LONGUEVILLE to JOLIMETZ (11 miles thereabout).	A/M
JOLIMETZ				
	23rd		Brigade Commander inspected the billets of the Batt", assisted on the recorded clerk by the A.A.9.	A/M
	24th		Q.M.G. 50th Div.	
			SALVAGE	
			The only salvage carried out this month has been a large shell dump at MAUBEUGE during the period 13th to 25th.	A/M
			DEMOBILISATION	
			The following were demobilised this month. 3 Offrs and 206 O.R.s in accordance to "3"	A/M
			Reg. Soldiers with more than 3 years to serve who were sent home.	A/M
			STRENGTH	
			31.1.19 4.2 Officers 610 O.R.	
			28.2.19 39 " 392 "	

R.G. Soames Lt Col.
4 KRRC

4th BN. THE KINGS ROYAL RIFLE CORPS.

WAR DIARY
or
INTELLIGENCE SUMMARY.

(Erase heading not required.)

MARCH, 1919.
Vol. V. No 4.

Place	Date	Hour	Summary of Events and Information	Remarks and references to Appendices
JOLIMETZ			During this month demobilisation proceeded regularly. Cadre Strength being reached by the end of the month. The salvage of the area allotted to the Bn was completed.	
			2/Lt Chadwick was attached to run in the trials for the B.E.F. Cross Country Race. Field-Marshal Sir Douglas Haig visited le Quesnoy), the Commanding Officer being present at) the Conference.	HM
	13.		Warning Order for Cadre to be ready to proceed to England after 16th inst (cancelled on 14th inst) HM 18th Bn The Kings Royal Rifle Corps (2nd Army) = Strength 10 Offrs	HM
	24.		Rhine Draft proceeded to join 18th Bn The Kings Royal Rifle Corps (2nd Army) = Strength 10 Offrs 170 O.Rs.	HM
	30		The Battalion was reduced to Cadre 'A' strength.	HM
			Demobilisation	
			The following were demobilised this month. 6 Offrs + 208 O.Rs in addition to 1 wafted Draft 2 Officers proceeded to U.K. on 2 months leave + 8 O.Rs with more than 2 years service to do	HM
			Strength	
			28. 2.19 39 Officers 392 O.Rs.	
			31. 3.19 18 97	

H.S.A. Kean Lt Col
The Kings Royal Rifle Corps
Comdg 4th Bn

4th Bn. The King's Royal Rifle Corps

L K R P C
April 1919

WAR DIARY
or
INTELLIGENCE SUMMARY.
(Erase heading not required.)

Vol. V. No 5.

Army Form C. 2118.

Instructions regarding War Diaries and Intelligence Summaries are contained in F. S. Regs., Part II. and the Staff Manual respectively. Title pages will be prepared in manuscript.

Place	Date	Hour	Summary of Events and Information	Remarks and references to Appendices
Jolimetz	7		The Bn. has been awaiting orders to proceed to England. Owing to being at Cadre Strength - no work carried out this month.	
	11	08:30	Lt. Col. Soames proceeded to England on leave - Capt. R.G.C. Disbrow took over command of the Bn. 2nd Bn. K.R.Rif. Corps arrived - in the next week all the Bn. Stores were handed over to 2nd Bn.	
			Demobilisation The following were demobilised this month - 2 Offrs. 2 O.Rs. to U.K. on 3 months leave on re-enlistment Strength	
			31-3-19 18 Offrs 97 O.Rs. 30-4-19 10 " 53 "	

R.J.A Kent Lt Col
The King's Royal Rifle Corps
Commdg 4th Bn.

WAR DIARY
or
INTELLIGENCE SUMMARY.

Army Form C. 2118.

4th Bn K. Royal Rifle Corps

Vol V No 6

MAY 1919

Place	Date	Hour	Summary of Events and Information	Remarks and references to Appendices
JOLIMETZ			Owing to Bn now being at reduced Cadre Strength of 5 Officers + 36 O.Rs no more has been carried out this month	AM
	11		Col. W.J. Soames ceases to command the Bn on posting to Russian Relief Force	AM
	30		Warning Order for Cadre to proceed to AINTREE received.	AM
			Demobilisation	
			The following men demobilised this month —	AM
			1 Officer	
			in addition 3 O.Rs to U.K. on leave — re-engaged + 7 O.Rs posted to 18th Bn K.R.Rif.C.	AM
			Strength	
			30 - 4 -19 10 Offrs 53 O.Rs	
			31 - 5 -19 4 33	

Comdg. 4 KRRC
The King's Royal Rifle Corps

H.Q. The Kings Royal Rifle Corps to date of embarkation June 1919

Army Form C. 2118.

WAR DIARY
or
INTELLIGENCE SUMMARY.
(Erase heading not required.)

JUNE 1919
Vol I No 1

Instructions regarding War Diaries and Intelligence Summaries are contained in F. S. Regs., Part II. and the Staff Manual respectively. Title pages will be prepared in manuscript.

Place	Date	Hour	Summary of Events and Information	Remarks and references to Appendices
JOLIMETZ	2	15.00	Cadre of H.Q. entrained for Le Havre & proceeded to AIRAINES	
	3	20.00	" " " " " arrived at Le Havre & proceeded to Honfleur Despatching Camp	
	7	17.30	Cadre embarked on S.S. St George for Southampton	
			Strength of Cadre at time of Embarkation	
			Offrs — 4	
			O.Rs — 33	

P.H.W. Westmoreland Lt.
The Kings Royal Rifle Corps
Comdg H "I.B"

www.ingramcontent.com/pod-product-compliance
Lightning Source LLC
Chambersburg PA
CBHW081450160426
43193CB00013B/2432